Cover illustration: *Winchester Mystery House.*
Courtesy of
Winchester Mystery House
525 South Winchester Boulevard
San Jose, California.

Portions of this book originally appeared in somewhat different form
in *Haunted Houses and Wandering Ghosts.* San Francisco Examiner
Division of the Hearst Corporation. Special Projects.

Revised Edition.
Fourth Printing September, 1998

WIDE WORLD PUBLISHING/ TETRA
P.O. Box 476
San Carlos, CA 94070

Library of Congress Cataloging –in–Publication Data
May, Antoinette.
    Haunted houses of California : a ghostly guide / by Antoinette
    May.
            p.   cm.
    Includes bibliographical references.
ISBN 0-933174-91-8 : $10.95
        1. Haunted houses--California.   2. Ghosts--California.
    3. California--Description and travel--Guide-books.   I. Title.
    BF1472.U6M39   1993
    133. 1'09794--dc20   90-12758
                                                                    CIP

HAUNTED HOUSES

of California

by ANTOINETTE MAY

**A GHOSTLY GUIDE TO HAUNTED HOUSES
AND WANDERING SPIRITS**

WIDE WORLD PUBLISHING/TETRA

To two great ghost chasers—
Sylvia Brown and Nick Nocerino

and to

C.J. Marrow and Vern Appleby
who made the chase a merry one.

TABLE OF CONTENTS

From Ghoulies and
Ghosties and
Tong-leggety Beasties
And things that Go
Bump in the Night
Good Lord Deliver Us!

—Scottish prayer

FORWARD

Antoinette May and I have known each other for twenty years. During that time we have spent many pleasant and sometimes harrowing times in haunted houses and places throughout the state. I have known her as a dear and respected friend. More important, I am fully aware of her work as a thorough reporter and researcher. She approaches everything with a needed skepticism, as well as an open mind.

We have spent cold nights and thankless nights in many a forbidding house, such as the Winchester Mystery House or the Toys 'R Us store with the hope of releasing some wounded lost soul.

Antoinette, with some wonderful infused psychic sense of her own, seems to know how to ask the right questions of the medium working, so she can piece the story and events together and not only make it wonderful reading, but an accurate account of what is taking place now and then.

Antoinette's work spans at least two decades that I know of and psychically, I feel she has not even come into her full excellence. With this book and the ones to come, she is certainly achieving it. I love Toni, and you will too. This woman, who has more courage than most, has a pen truly mightier than any sword I've seen.

— Sylvia Brown

All houses wherein men
have lived and died
Are haunted houses.

— Henry Wadworth Longfellow

INTRODUCTION

I used to like ghost stories. The scarier the better. But always when the story was over, my goose bumps receding, the hair on my head lying flat again, I'd invariably laugh and say, "Naturally no sensible person *believes* in such things.

I used to say that anyway. Now I'm not so sure.

In the past eighteen years of investigating alleged hauntings, I've discovered that psychically speaking California is loaded and apparently always has been.

The events are commonly connected with a certain space — usually a house. They consist of poltergeist activity — unexplained disturbances such as sounds, smells, the movement of objects or temperature changes — or hallucinatory experiences, such as seeing "ghosts."

The parapsychologists who investigate these stories believe that hauntings and poltergeist phenomena — if verifiable — indicate an untapped energy source and, more importantly, survival of the human soul.

In searching out potential haunts, human investigators may be drawn to Charles Addams Victorians with their long, dark corridors, widow's walks, and dramatic staircases. But the ghosts themselves show a profound indifference to such things.

The ghost, it seems, is concerned with *what* happened to him or her, not where it happened. In most accounts of hauntings, the spirit comes back to erase, re-enact, avenge or simply brood about some awful event or unfulfilled longing. The spirit of Manuela Girardin, for instance, is said to hover about the room of her ailing grandchildren. Mrs. Girardin fell sick and died while tending the children more than one hundred years ago. Visitors to the historic Stevenson house in Monterey frequently reported glimpsing her ghostly form.

Another lingering spirit is said to be that of Juanita, lynched by a gang of angry Gold Rush miners in retaliation for her having killed a member of their band who had raped her. The tragedy will never be forgotten as long as Juanita returns to haunt the Downieville bridge where she was hanged.

Other spirits seem inclined to continue in more comfortable earthly patterns. What a devoted homemaker Anna Whaley must have been if in death she still returns to her home in San Diego just to check on things!

That California with its riotous history and unresolved conflicts would inspire a legion of restless spirits is not surprising. Even before statehood, Californians talked of a phantom cow, an apparition that wandered Yerba Buena Island, mooing mournfully over the loss of its calf which had been barbecued by pirates. During Gold Rush days Mark Twain wrote of his encounter with the Kearny Street ghost, an apparition that confronted many early San Franciscans.

In December 1871, several thousand curious people flocked to another San Francisco location—the widow Jorgenson's house on Mason Street—where a bodiless head appeared at a second story window. The floating visage manifested itself at random day or night.

Reporters described a sorrowful face with a goatee, droopy mustache and longish, wavy hair. Though Mrs. Jorgenson disagreed, many felt that it resembled her late husband. Eventually the whole window was removed and taken for observation to a judge's office. The face followed. Later both were acquired by Woodward's Gardens, a popular restaurant. After a time the phantom face simply faded away.

Soon after, a group of poker players, gathered at the home of J. J. Hucks, looked up from their game to see another floating face—this time an elderly man with a long, bulbous nose—peering at them through an upper story window. Hucks walked fearlessly to the window and yanked down the shade. Apparently rebuffed, the specter did not return.

A more recent example of the same phenomenon was investigated by PSI (Psychic Science Investigators), a group of researchers based in Fullerton.

PSI was called in when the visage of a Neanderthal-like man appeared in the mirror of a trailer parked in the Tahoe area. What was it? Where did it come from? Why did it appear? Nobody was quite sure. Members of the research team were able to successfully photograph the image which remains on the mirror today—despite numerous attempts to remove it.

PSI organized in 1973 to investigate psychic phenomena and has since visited literally hundreds of houses, museums and graveyards. Much evidence has been collected including a tape made at the San Juan Capistrano Cemetery of a voice that whispers breathily, "I want to give you my name," Another tape recorded message from a graveyard seance says quite distinctly, "I'm scared."

Though the spirits may be frightened, the researchers definitely are not. Harry Shepherd, a leader of the group, speaks casually of a band of spirits who have seemingly attached themselves to his family. "I see them at night around the bed just as I drop off," he says. There are five of them and if I don't see them all just before dozing off I know that something's wrong. One night I noticed that one was missing and got up to check the house. Sure enough—a gas burner had been left on."

Not long after forming PSI, Chris and Norm Metzner became aware of "Fred," a spectral roommate whose reactions are very much of this world. Using a pasteboard box or card table as a means of demonstrating energy, the spirit responds visibly to the clink of glasses or the presence of a pretty woman. This entity responds to human encouragement and has been known to lift a table completely off the floor in full view of twenty people.

One of the best known psychic investigators in California is F. R. "Nick" Nocerino, who has been involved in paranormal research for more than forty years. A gifted medium, Nocerino has the ability to actually photograph spirits. Among the hundreds of pictures he has taken are

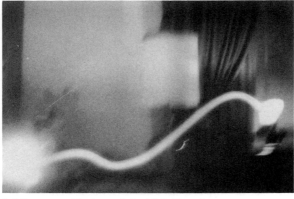

Spirit energy.   Photograph by Nick Nocerino.

blobs, lightning-like bolts or shafts of white light, and actual faces and forms of what appear to be discarnate entities. Some of the images are clear and distinct, while others are vague outlines. In some as yet unexpected way, Nocerino and his associate, Chuck Pelton, are able to act as catalysts between the spirit or energy form and the light-sensitive film.

To take their extraordinary pictures, Nocerino and Pelton use ordinary cameras, Pentax Honeywells with Tri-X 400 ASA film and no light. "We try to forget about the mechanics of picture taking," Nocerino says, "and shut off our conscious minds. What we get in our pictures is sheer energy—spirit energy."

While accompanying Nick on some of his field trips, I've observed him take pictures of "things" invisible to the naked eye while at other times his camera was unable to photograph a phantom "light show" seen by many. This paradox seems common to all psychic photographers.

Nocerino has responded to thousands of requests for investigations — and sometimes exorcisms–of reportedly haunted houses. Photographing the premises is an integral part

Nick Nocerino doing psychometry..   Photograph by C.J. Marrow.

of the investigation. Packaged film is unsealed on the spot and later developed commercially.

Nick Nocerino and A. May. Photograph by C. J. Marrow.

Of course all the ordinary explanations for apparent spirit photography are considered: faulty equipment, double exposure, light leaks or reflections, faulty development, refractions and, naturally the possible delusion of the viewer. Any or all of these could account for the "spirit." After discounting for these possibilities, some pictures remain that can only be explained in supernatural terms.

In 1975, Dr. Jules Eisenbud, then clinical professor of psychiatry at the University of Colorado Medical School, says that since 1861 more than two dozen persons in several countries have claimed to obtain on photographic plates and film a variety of types of images that could only have been produced paranormally. I would tend to place the figure much higher.

How might such apparitions—on film or otherwise—be created? The most intriguing explanation is delayed telepathy. Assume that one experiences a severe shock such as witnessing or receiving word of a death. Immediately an image is created which may be intense enough to cause it to be "set" in time at a particular wave length. Possibly years later, an individual whose receiver is tuned to the same wave length is confronted with that image—and a ghost is born.

Judging from the number of individuals reporting spectral contact, one doesn't have to be a professional medium to see a ghost. They attract believer and nonbeliever indiscriminately. What seems to be required is the ability to tune into the electromagnetic field or "vibes." How many may have the ability to do this without even being aware of it?

To be a ghost hunter one needs only a rational outlook, a good memory, a sense of humor and an inquisitive, flexible mind. Basic equipment begins with a notebook and pencil—tape recorders, thermometers, cameras and geiger counters to be acquired as interest increases.

If nothing paranormal occurs while you're visiting the houses described here, you will have lost nothing. As an adventure in historical research, haunted houses have no equal.

As for the phenomena of haunting itself, there's certainly nothing new about it. Ghost stories were popular in Roman times. Pliny wrote about spirits nearly two thousand years ago and there is indication that cave dwellers decorated their walls with pictures of spirits.

In the 16th Century, Emperor Maximillian of Austria called out the army to ensure that there would be no ghosts in the hotels in which he planned to stay. Some two hundred years later Dr. Samuel Johnson observed to his friend and biographer, James Boswell, "It is wonderful that six thousand years have now elapsed since the creation of the world and still it is undecided whether or not there has ever been an instance of the spirit of any person appearing after death. All argument is against it, all belief is for it."

Recently 17,000 persons were queried by the British Society for Psychical Research. In answer to the question, "Have you ever, when believing yourself to be completely awake, had a vivid impression of seeing or being touched by a being or inanimate object, or of hearing a voice which was not due to any physical cause?" nearly 1700, or 10 percent, answered YES.

Perhaps the strongest explanation for the ghost's continued popularity is its implied optimism. A spirit has literally conquered death and come back to prove it. It is both a clue and an invitation to a world beyond our own limited reality, an offer to broaden our awareness to encompass everything and anything that just might be possible.

And who can ignore that kind of challenge?

Antoinette May
Palo Alto, California

I do not feel myself
authorized to reject all
ghost stories; for however
improbable one taken
alone might appear, the
mass of them taken
together command credence.

— Immanual Kant

NORTHERN CALIFORNIA

THE EASKOOT HOUSE

Surely the most ghostly ghost around is Captain Alfred Easkoot, who wanders the misty shores of Marin on stormy nights searching, searching searching for his golden hook.

In life, Easkoot had a withered hand to which a golden hook was fixed. In death, as his casket was carried across the sand, the hook somehow became detached and was washed out to sea.

It would be hard to find a more classic example of folk fantasy and yet there are many over the years who claim to have seen the shadowy form of the old sea captain silhouetted against the dunes of Stinson Beach. Still more have testified to poltergeist phenomena in the captain's house.

Alfred Derby Easkoot was born in Manchester, Massachusetts, on Feb. 3, 1820. At the age of nine, he went to sea as a cabin boy. Fours years later he was severely injured in a fire at sea that scarred his face and turned one hand into a withered claw.

After his recovery, young Easkoot went back to sea, eventually becoming a ship's captain and master of a merchant ship sailing between Philadelphia and South America. Later Captain Easkoot's own lumber schooner went aground on Duxbury Reef near Stinson Beach. He survived the wreck and built a house from the remnants that washed ashore, then went on to become Marin County's first surveyor and a successful business man.

He lived alone and apparently content until he fell in love with Amelia Dumas, a wealthy and stylish Philadelphian. How the crusty old salt managed to woo and wed a beautiful and elegant woman with the romantic name of of Amelia is another mystery, but he did.

The captain's snug cabin was torn down and redesigned to suit the taste of his eastern bride. The original timbers may still be seen in the stairway of the graceful New England Colonial.

Easkoot made wise land investments and ten years after his wedding in 1871, retired from surveying and established a resort-campground called Easkoot's Beach, where the public beach is today.

Easkoot House as it is today. Photograph by Vern Appleby.

The captain was a beloved figure among vacationers at the beach. He took visitors on fishing trips, played with children and presided over sing-a-longs and taffy pulls.

Life went well for Easkoot until 1886 when Amelia rose from the dinner table in great pain and collapsed. She died in Easkoot's arms. There were rumors of foul play by the captain, but an autopsy revealed that she'd died of a ruptured heart.

Easkoot was alone again but no longer contented with his lot. The once outgoing businessman became an embittered recluse who patrolled the beach with a spyglass searching for trespassers. The proud manor house was allowed to fall into disrepair until it was almost obscured by vines and bushes. It's said that it was at this time that the captain affixed a golden hook to his withered hand.

NORTHERN CALIFORNIA

Competition developed between Easkoot and Nathan Stinson—the Point Reyes dairy farmer for whom the town was named—for the area's seashore business. The rivalry became an obsession that absorbed Easkoot until his death of a heart attack on December 10, 1905.

That Easkoot's home would eventually become the property of a Stinson—Eve Stinson Fitzhenry—seems the final irony.

The house enjoyed a brief renaissance during Mrs. Fitzhenry's ownership in the 1930s. Charming gardens were planted and groves of trees—now grown tall, totally concealing the house and blocking the sea view as well. It was during this period that stories began to circulate concerning the place. Doors opened and closed at their own volition. Lights flashed on and off of their own accord. There were unexplainable cold spots and smells. Tales were told of the shadowy figure of a man with a loose, dangling sleeve and a seaman's cap.

It was feared that the captain's soul was tormented, doomed to search forever for his hook. Residents said that every night at 2, the hour of his death, Captain Easkoot came stomping into his home.

A couple who occupied the house were awakened one night by their bed's fierce shaking. Horrified, they saw a shadowy figure leering at them from the foot of the bed—a whiskered gentleman with a seaman's cap and a dangling sleeve. The phantom waved the sleeve, gurgled incoherently, and walked away on creaking shoes.

Soon after, they heard heavy footsteps on the walnut staircase followed by violent thumps against the hollow walls of the attic.

Not surprisingly the house was sold and resold, changing hands several times.

Then in March of 1976 great clouds of smoke were seen pouring from the house. The blaze gutted parts of the interior, blackened the outside and destroyed thousands of dollars worth of antiques and paintings. Fortunately no one was in the house at the time. Rumors are rampant

The Easkoot House immediately after the fire.   Photograph by C.J. Marrow

but the official fire report, accepted by the insurance company, lists the cause as a defective electric heater. Though many belongings remained about the charred house, the tenants never returned. Their whereabouts are still unknown.

In 1984, Leonard Chapman, personnel manager with the Southern Pacific Transportation Co., and his wife, Judy , dean of students at Dominican College, and their daughter Renata, then, 14, bought the house.

"I know the place has a reputation for being haunted," Chapman told Kevin Leary, a reporter for the *San Francisco Chronicle*, "but I've never seen the ghost. If we have one, I'm sure he's a happy ghost and I'd like to meet him."

"Oh, a few things have happened since we moved in, but they're all explainable — just about."

Maybe so, but Cinno, the family's 100-pound malamute, apparently

NORTHERN CALIFORNIA

doesn't agree. When brought into the house, the hackles of the usually mild mannered dog went up. She dug in her paws and tried to jump out the window, leaving claw marks on the sill. Cinno, a former house dog, now prefers to sleep outside.

A few days after the family moved in, and before their new burglar alarm was hooked up, the alarm bell began ringing for no apparent reason.

"We have an expensive and sophisticated system—it had not been connected and yet there it was ringing at 2 a. m.," Chapman recalls.

He ran up to the attic and tried to disconnect the wires, but the alarm just kept ringing. "I was hugging the bell trying to smother the sound so it wouldn't wake the neighbors; but nothing helped. Then it just shut off by itself after about ten minutes."

Then the action seemed to focus on Renata. She was doing her homework in her bedroom when a scratching noise suddenly began to emanate from under the bed. Renata peered beneath the spread but saw nothing. Then unaccountably the mattress began bouncing up and down.

And so the legend continues. It's easy to imagine that the misanthropic captain continues to view trespassers with hostility. At night when fog shrouds the coast and whitecaps dot the swirling surf, lights may flicker unaccountably inside the house. "Maybe it's the captain," someone invariably suggests.

And who is to say he's wrong?

The Easkoot house, a private home, is located at 3548 Shoreline Highway in Stinson Beach.

THE HAUNTED DOLL HOUSE

When Charlene Weber purchased a century-old house in Bodega, a parting remark from the former owners was the wish that she liked ghosts.

In 1974 ghosts were the last thing Weber had on her mind. She was busy with plans to open an antique shop and doll museum. If she thought of anything weird it was the town of Bodega itself with its memories of Alfred Hitchcock's thriller *The Birds*. Everywhere Weber looked she was reminded of a horrifying scene from the movie filmed there.

Charlene's Country Treasures. .Photograph by A. May.

Fortunately the local birds behaved themselves and Weber began to acquire and display her dolls. These range from one half inch to human size. The most bizarre is a life-size effigy of an eight year old girl. As the child lay in her coffin a death mask was made of her face. From this an exact likeness was created and applied to the head of a doll. Before burial, the little girl's long blond hair, eyelashes and eyebrows were removed and attached to the doll's head.

The doll survived the child's grieving parents and on their death joined Charlene Weber's amazing collection. One night not long after she acquired the doll, Weber was awakened by the sound of a zither playing and then a loud crashing noise. Following the eerie music to the second floor, she found the floor littered with broken glass from the case that had housed the effigy doll.

As she surveyed the doll, Weber realized to her horror that the perpetually smiling expression had given way to one of incredible sadness. Even more amazing was a tiny drop of moisture below one blue eye. Could it have been a tear?

Returning the next morning with a friend, Weber discovered that the doll was not in its usual place. Instead of resting on its customary pedestal, it now stood in the middle of the room. The sad expression of the previous night was gone. Once again the face was lifeless—except for the eyes. The eyes were focused on Weber following her every movement.

Though Charlene Weber has never seen a ghost herself, her guests and customers have. Again and again a visitor will describe a tall man wearing Victorian clothes who bears a striking resemblance to Abraham Lincoln. Some describe the same man dressed in what appears to be a naval uniform. Often he's glimpsed bending over what looks like a child's bed.

Invited to conduct a seance in the house, medium Sylvia Brown made contact with a spirit who identified himself as a sea captain. His name was McCuen, he told her. The spirit spoke of a sick child and appeared to resent the intrusion of strangers in his home.

Later Weber did some research and discovered that a McCuen family had indeed lived in the house nearly one hundred years ago. Even more revealing, there had been a brain damaged child confined to a crib.

At least one guest feels that the old captain takes his proprietorship of the house a bit too far. She was using the bathroom in the museum when the door opened and an apparition of a Lincolnesque man confronted her. She screamed and the man vanished.

Who knows, perhaps the spirit was embarrassed too.

Charlene's Country Treasures is located on Bodega Road just past the Salmon Creek Bridge. The shop and museum are open to the public on weekends from 9 to 5. Telephone: (707) 876-3104.

VALLEY OF THE MOON SALOON

There are spirits and then there are spirits, obviously not all are found in bottles. Carolina Ceelen, owner of the Valley of the Moon Saloon, is certain of that.

Ceelan says that she's had numerous close encounters—of the spooky kind—and seen enough apparitions in the two room, 100 year old bar to *know* the place is haunted.

Several customers, the upstairs tenant, and a few employees are equally sure — and they all insist that this isn't the kind of spirit that appears only after a stiff belt or a few beers.

Carolina Ceelan. Photograph by A. May.

It all began with records that inexplicably popped out of their secured slots in the juke box. Then the sound of pool balls hitting one another was heard when no one was playing—no one human, that is. Money in the cash register which had been carefully counted, sorted and bound with rubber bands was found strewn about the drawer, yet none was missing. Several patrons sat spellbound as they watched bicycles stored in the back room suddenly sway back and forth only to stop abruptly as if someone or some*thing* has grabbed them.

David Wooster, who occupies the apartment above the saloon, was a bit dubious about moving in when the former tenant told him of a bar of soap that just floated into his hand while he showered one morning—as though some obliging soul had handed it to him. But the cheap rent convinced him to take a chance and he hasn't been sorry.

Valley of the Moon Saloon. Photograph by A. May.

"The ghost isn't a bad roommate," he says. "It's pretty much live and let live—or something like that; but he does have one idiosyncrasy. It's the pantry door. He wants it closed. When I forget, he has a way of letting me know. Suddenly lights go on and off by themselves and things get moved from one room to another."

One afternoon Carolina Ceelen was alone in the pub waiting for the beer distributor, when the ghost touched her arm. Another time it gently patted her posterior.

What can one conclude about this ghost that may—or may not—be a carry over from the Indian burial grounds that once comprised the area?

Perhaps this is an easy-going kind of spirit. He appears to enjoy the small town pub atmosphere with its clutter of video games, wooden stools and walls covered with mirrors, posters and neon lights all advertising beer. Apparently he enjoys being where the action is and occasionally can't restrain himself from being a part of it.

Surely one thing is certain: this ghost is still human enough to enjoy the companionship of a very pretty woman.

The Valley of the Moon Saloon is located at 17154 Sonoma Highway, Sonoma. Telephone: (707) 996-4003

NORTHERN CALIFORNIA

THE MADRONO MANOR: The Ghost & Mrs. Muir

They call them painted ladies—those fragile old Victorians gussied up in bright colors, held together by prayers. It was just such a structure that seemed a dream come true to Carol Muir.

While in Saudi Arabia, Carol and her husband, John, a Bechtel executive, had dreamed of becoming innkeepers. Fantasy took a quantum leap toward reality when the couple put last things first. While vacationing in Nepal, Carol and John visited a rosewood factory where, "on an impulse" they placed an order for ten tables, forty chairs, ten mirror frames, trim for forty doors and one magnificent front door. Now they *had* to do it!

Returning to California, they proceeded to search for the "perfect house." Cruelly, it eluded them. No place was right until one day Carol came to the slumbering town of Healdsburg where, quite by chance, peeking through a locked iron gate she caught a glimpse of John Paxton's mansion.

Healdsburg has always been a place where days move quietly. In Paxton's time it was known as the buckle of Sonoma's prosperous prunebelt.

Today, although the town is surrounded by three internationally known vineyards, it appears strangely unaware of its new found popularity. The unpretentious charm of this "in" spot is like the modesty of a young duckling suddenly discovering itself a swan.

Surveying a Gothic Victorian mansion with its wraparound veranda and mansard roof, Carol wondered about the former occupants. Who had walked within those walls, loving, laughing, crying? What angry words were spoken there? As she spoke with oldtimers and searched Sonoma County records, a family saga emerged. The property was acquired in

1879 by John Alexander Paxton, a state legislator who, having made a fortune in mining, banking, lumber, was ready to turn his attention to Sonoma's fledgling wine industry.

Madrono Manor

Townspeople were awed by the entrepreneur and watched fascinated as his grand mansion, set on a knoll surrounded by towering trees took form.   In 1880 the showplace was complete and a year later Paxton purchased the 40 acre Sterling Ranch where he established a thriving winery. Then, in 1887, Hannah Paxton received word that her husband had died of a sudden heart attack on a steamer while returning from a business trip to Liverpool.   The body was returned to Hannah who is said to have kept it in a leadlined, glass coffin *in the house* until her own death in 1902.

The couple's two sons, Blitz and Charles, inherited the dynasty. Blitz, who took over the family home as well as the presidency of the Bank of Santa Rosa, shocked the community by deserting his wife and their two

NORTHERN CALIFORNIA

children to marry another woman. Charles took his life after his wife deserted him for another man. The Paxton mansion was sold in 1913 and passed from one owner to another until it at last stood empty and waiting.

Carol Muir's first inkling that the house just might be haunted came early in 1982 shortly after she and her husband had purchased it. A crew of carpenters from Red Bluff would drive down late Sunday, working and camping in the house until their return home on Friday. "None of them saw anything, but all spoke of feeling a *presence*," she recalls. "Later some of the staff felt a sense of being watched and guests complained of things being moved to strange, unexpected places. I thought it was nonsense."

That was before Carolyn Yarbrough and her article in the *Los Angeles Times*. "There isn't much to do in Healdsburg or Madrona Manor after dinner," Yarbrough wrote in an account published in 1985. "Night falls like a great black curtain over the entire estate. Guests dawdle as long as possible over dinner and after dinner liqueurs."

But, as Yarbrough went on to describe to her readers, there would be a thrill she hadn't bargained for before the night was through.

Retiring to room 101 she fell asleep almost immediately, but awakened suddenly to confront a woman, possibly in her mid- 30s, wearing a long black dress, a narrow black ribbon fastening her white Peter Pan collar.

"I closed my eyes," the reporter wrote, "forcing myself to breathe more slowly. When I felt more in control, I opened my eyes with fearful trepidation. The woman had moved and was sitting in the blue velvet chair by the window. 'What do you want?' I asked. There was no answer and as I watched, straining to make out more details, the slender form dissolved."

The phenomenon was the topic of much speculation at breakfast the next morning. Though many scoffed, a waitress appeared merely surprised.

"Actually," she pointed out, "you weren't even in the haunted room. It's 201 where all the strange things have been happening."

Room 101, Madrono Manor

On June 19, 1986 Bill and SanDee Partirdge of Buena Park, California, were guests at the Madrona Manor. Upon completing their dinner, SanDee was startled to see one of the French doors open and a small gray haired lady dressed in the clothing of the last century enter the room. No one else was aware of her, but as SanDee continued to stare, the woman approached. "I'm glad that you can see me," she said. "I feel so badly sometimes that no one can. This was my house once and I like what's been done to it. I'd like to tell someone that—now you can tell them."

At first SanDee couldn't bring herself to discuss what had happened. Her husband had been sitting beside her the entire time and had seen nothing; but when she returned home, SanDee felt compelled to write to Carol Muir confiding her experience.

NORTHERN CALIFORNIA

Madrono Manor

And as for Mrs. Muir, what does she think about her ghost?   "Well, things do happen," she admitted to me. "Once at breakfast a woman literally shrieked because a coffee cup revolved on its saucer right before her eyes. It's hard to ignore *that* kind of evidence. Recently guests from Santa Barbara, Dean Mars, a well known sculptor, and his wife, Melinda, presented me with crystal chips accompanied by elaborate instructions for placing them in holes marking the four corners of the property. These 'sentinels" would guard and protect me, they explained. I followed the advice — it could hardly do any harm."

Attractive, gregarious, highly efficient, this Mrs. Muir, unlike her fey movie namesake, would rather brag about her son's cooking—Todd, a graduate of the California Culinary Academy, worked at the famed Chez Panisse Restaurant before coming to the Madrona—or discuss the inn's extensive prize winning wine list, than ponder ghostly possibilities.

"If you can say live and let live about a ghost, that's how I feel," she explains. "I don't bother them—they don't bother me. We're all happy."

The Madrona Manor is located at 1001 Westside Road, Healdsburg, CA 95448. Phone: (707)433-4231

NORTHERN CALIFORNIA

MIGLIAVACCA MANSION

Perhaps only an inmate on Death Row awaiting a last minute reprieve could fully appreciate the tale of the Migliavacca Mansion.

Condemned to demolition, facing certain destruction again and again, the historic landmark in downtown Napa has clung tenuously to life, one last minute stay of execution after another, delaying the inevitable.

Many fine Victorians have endured similar cliffhangers in recent years. But the Magiliavacca house is not just another Victorian. Not only is it an integral part of Napa Valley's living legend, but it possesses a spirit that stubbornly refuses to vacate the premises—despite the fact that the building itself has been moved twice.

The story has its beginnings in 1833 with the birth of Giacomo Migliavacca in Italy. Migrating to the United States as a boy, he settled in Napa, opening a small grocery store in 1867. Soon the store was known for its fine wine selection and before long Migliavacca was creating his own varieties. What began as a bathtub venture grew and prospered, and in 1880 land was purchased and a winery constructed. Giacomo, his wife, Marie, and their children — eventually numbering thirteen — lived upstairs.

In 1895 work began on their impressive Queen Anne mansion; a lighter, airier design which had developed as an alternative to the starker, more Gothic lines of the classic English Victorian. Constructed of the finest materials available, the house reflected essential Queen Anne elements—rounded tower, steep gabled roof and varied textures—at their loveliest. The upper two stories were imported Italian slate shingles over redwood sheeting and the prominent corner turret had a slate roof and curved windows. Stained glass windows were another prominent feature. The first floor consisted of a front parlor, sitting room and reception hall complete with a "coachman's corner," where visitor's coachmen awaited their employers. An oak staircase led to the second floor with its center hallway, five bedrooms and full Victorian bath. The third floor was designed as a grand ballroom. All trim was handcarved redwood, with the exception of the handcarved oak reception area. The details and quality of materials make modern architectural duplication virtually impossible.

The Migliavacca Mansion. Photograph by Vern Appleby.

After Giacomo Migliavacca's death, his son James became a director of the Bank of Italy, later to become the Bank of America. Another son, Laurence, took over the family winery. With the death of Angelina in 1921, last member of the immediate family, the once proud mansion sank into a genteel decline standing empty until finally sold by the family in 1925.

During World War II, the second and third floors were divided into small sleeping rooms to house Mare Island employees. Among them was Anna Wurz and her family. They complained often to Jess Doud, now executive director of the Napa County Historical Society, that the house was haunted. Night after night the Wurz family, occupying the top floor—formerly the ballroom—was awakened by the sound of footsteps approaching them on the stairs. Opening the door, they were confronted by darkness. There were other sounds too: laughter and old fashioned music. The Wurz family wanted to leave, but housing was in short supply during the war.

When the world conflict ended, the house stood empty. There were other owners but no one ever remained for long. Then in 1970, the property was purchased by Napa County for $20,400 and demolition was scheduled to make way for a new library. At the last minute, Trost Housemovers came to the rescue. The house was jacked up and moved one block to the bank of the Napa River, awaiting a barge trip to a new location in Benicia.

Bureaucratic roadblocks shattered that hope. Benicia didn't want a "potential fire trap—least of all one with a ghost." Another potential buyer surfaced with plans to relocate the house a short distance down river. More redtape strangled that idea.

Meanwhile the Migliavacca house in its isolated riverside location was an easy mark for vandals and looters who used chain saws to remove the staircase and light fixtures. Many preservationists questioned whether a professional demolition job wasn't preferable to a slow, torturous death. Jackals of the night were literally tearing the house to pieces.

Condemned once more, a last minute reprieve was sought by Tom Connell. Young, inexperienced, idealistic—Connell resolved to do the job that had totally defied the so-called experts. In 1975, he moved the Magliavacca house for a second time, selecting a lot close to its original location. Full of confidence, he predicted that the mansion would be fully restored within six months. In reality, the project took three years. Often work ground to a total stop, the building standing forlornly, smothered by scaffolding, interior gutted.

But Connell's perseverance paid off. Today the Magiliavacca Mansion is again a showplace and has been listed on the National Register of Historic Places. Once more the building radiates Victorian splendor — though the top floor is no longer used as a ballroom, nor do coachmen wait in the front hallway.   Divided into seven offices, the mansion now houses myriad interests. Laughter is anything but eerie, cheerful voices echo through the halls, brisk footsteps are heard.

But at night. . . .well no one ever really likes to work too late.........

The Migliavacca Mansion is located at 1417 Fourth Street, Napa, Ca.

NORTHERN CALIFORNIA

True love is like ghosts,
which everybody talks about
and few have seen.

— François Duc de La Rochefoucauld

SAN FRANCISCO

THE HASKELL HOUSE

THE SAN FRANCISCO ART INSTITUTE

THE MONTANDON TOWNHOUSE

THE HAUNTING OF ALCATRAZ

THE MANSIONS HOTEL & RESTAURANT

THE HASKELL HOUSE

"Fire! . . . one. . . .two." In the time it took to say those three words, California's most famous duel occurred, the Broderick-Terry affair.

David C. Broderick

U.S. Senator David C. Broderick had been a New York saloonkeeper and Tammany henchman before coming to gold-rush San Francisco, according to his own accounts, "sick and penniless." Before long he was literally coining money—taking gold dust and turning it into five and ten dollar gold pieces at a handsome profit.

With health and finances improved, Broderick studied history, literature and law and was admitted to the bar; then ran for the state senate and became its president. By 1851 he was in absolute control of San Francisco's political machinery—adored by some, detested by others. One historian described Broderick as "the rudest, roughest, most aggressive young man in the area." The young politician made either friends who would die for him or enemies who would—if if was possible—cause him to die.

State Supreme Court Justice David S. Terry was equally pugnacious. When the two met for their fateful duel, he had only recently been released after stabbing a Vigilante officer.

The two men were fiercely divided on the issue of slavery. Terry, a Southerner steeped in the traditions of plantation society, was determined that California become a slave state. Broderick was equally determined that it would not.

Of all the free states, California had the most stringent laws against blacks. Shortly after achieving statehood, the California legislature enacted a law that virtually made slaves of freed blacks. Under the law a black man or woman could be brought before a magistrate and claimed as a fugitive. Since the seized individual was not permitted to testify, the judge had no alternative but to issue a certificate of ownership to the claimant.

Anyone who gave assistance to a fugitive was liable to a fine of five hundred dollars or imprisonment for two months. Slaves who had been brought to California by their masters before statehood, and had since been freed by a constitutional prohibition of slavery, were held to be fugitives and were liable to arrest although they may have been free for several years. Though it was obvious that the intention was as much to kidnap free blacks as it was to apprehend fugitives, the law was re-enacted year after year.

Outspoken criticism of the practice did little to endear Broderick to the many influential Southerners in government—Terry among them.

There was an angry exchange of words and then a challenge. The two would settle their dispute with a duel. Broderick spent the night prior to the fateful meeting with a close friend, Leonides K. Haskell at his charming bayside cottage near Black Point. It was clear to Haskell that his friend was in no condition to risk his life. He had just completed an exhausting political campaign in which his health had been a problem. The night before the duel he lay on the floor until the early hours of the morning drinking coffee and talking. Haskell said later that Broderick was "fey—all night," that is, a man deeply disturbed.

But in the morning Broderick smiled reassuringly as they climbed into the carriage that would take them to the appointed place, a farm near Lake Merced just over the San Mateo County line.

The behavior of the two parties was in sharp contrast as they met in the early morning sunlight. While Terry's seconds were cool and assured, Broderick's men were uncertain and inexperienced. Haskell partially removed Broderick's cravat and then, overcome with emotion, walked away and stood for a moment wringing his hands in anguish. Sadly he returned at last to finish his task.

Broderick's own confidence had returned and he looked out at the crowd of some eighty spectators who'd gathered, nodding to some.

A toss of a coin determined position and weapons to be used. Terry won and his pistols were produced and loaded. They were of Belgian make, eight-inch barrels which used Derringer-size balls and hair triggers. He had practiced often with them.

The gunsmith who loaded Broderick's pistol warned that the trigger was set too finely; it could be set off merely by a jerk or jar. His objections went unheeded. Broderick's hands changed position repeatedly as he tried to get the feel of the weapon.

The seconds stood back, leaving the principals to face one another from an ominous distance of twenty paces.

"Gentlemen, are you ready?"

"Yes," Terry replied promptly. Broderick hesitated an instant then nodded.

Both men shot between the words "fire" and "two." Broderick's bullet spent itself in the ground about nine feet in front of him. The weapon had fired as he raised it. Terry's bullet struck the senator in the chest, staggering him. For a moment Broderick stood erect, trying to brace himself and then fell backward onto the grass.

For a second the shots echoed in the still morning air. Then a half strangled cry came from the crowd, "That's murder, by God!" A surgeon hurried forward to stem the crimson flow that poured from the wound, while Terry remained erect, still in the classic stance of the duelist.

A wagon was brought and the senator was gently lifted and placed on a mattress within it. The party set off for the Haskell home retracing the route they'd taken just an hour before. Upon arrival Broderick was carried to a second floor bedroom which overlooked the sea. Physicians tended him around the clock. At first their reports were optimistic, then they changed as his condition worsened.

Broderick's sorrowing friends gathered around the bed. For three days their hopes rose and fell. At times Broderick conversed in heavy whispers, his body racked with pain. "They have killed me because I was opposed to extinction of slavery and a corrupt administration," he said at last. Shortly before midnight on September 16, 1857, Broderick lapsed into unconsciousness and at twenty minutes past nine the following morning he died.

In the hue and cry that arose over Broderick's death, the once powerful Southern faction heard its death knell. Broderick dead was a far more powerful man than Broderick living. A heretofore indifferent populace rallied around a martyr's grave. Perhaps Terry, in the thirty years before another man's bullet ended *his* life, had cause to ponder the paradoxical failure of a plan that succeeded.

But many think that death was not the end of the thirty-five-year-old senator. Surely Leonides Haskell must have felt the loss of his friend very keenly. It was in his home that Broderick had first received Terry's challenge, and the two were together constantly until Broderick's death six days later.

When Haskell's son was born a few months later, the child was named Broderick. The Haskell family remained in the house with its tragic memories until 1863 when the land was annexed by the military "for defense of San Francisco." This was the opening gun in a lengthy and complicated struggle between the government and Black Point property owners that hasn't been settled yet. Leonidas Haskell, who, during the Civil War, served as a major on General Fremont's staff, was in Washington still pressing his claim at the time of his death on January 15, 1873.

The Haskell House. Photograph by Vern Appleby.

Over the years a succession of tenants, military officers, have complained that the place was haunted. A man in a long black coat with a top hat has been seen many times pacing back and forth. Could this be Broderick reliving his anguish on the night before the duel? Many people have thought so.

Colonel Cecil Puckett, who lived in the house during the late 1970s, told of a presence in the kitchen. "I feel that something or someone follows me about the house at times," he said, "I even feel that it watches me in the shower."

Subsequent tenants continued to feel a presence. Capt. Jim Knight, (ret.) a recent MTMC Western Area deputy commander who lived in the house for two years, was certain that the house was haunted. "There's no doubt about it," he stated. "We didn't see or hear anything, but sometimes we'd be in the kitchen and the lights in the dining room would go on by themselves. Or we'd be downstairs and the john in the bathroom upstairs would flush by itself."

More eerie occurrences happened to Capt. Everett Jones, (ret.) who succeeded Knight in Quarters Three and lived there for three and a half years.

"After we moved in we had a couple of parties there and we joked about a ghost being in the house," Jones recalled. "One Saturday morning after a party, I was in the kitchen putting things away and heard a big crash. Upon investigating, I found that a picture with a picture hook and a nail an inch-and-a-half long had crashed to the floor. It didn't look like the nail had pulled out; it looked like someone had pushed it from behind.

"There was a similar incident later when five pictures fell off the same wall," Knight continued. "And my daughter was sitting on her bed one morning and one of those bolt-on light fixtures fell off without warning.

"There was no earthquake to account for it either," Knight added. "That all happened in the first six months after we moved in—we stopped joking about the ghost after that."

Capt. James W. Lunn, MTMC Western Area's present deputy commander, and his family live in Quarters Three now. Captain Lunn tells of going over to the house to check it out before moving in. "One of the painters said that he'd been working on the windows one day and *something* pushed him right out!"

Later the Lunn family saw plants tip over by themselves and shadows move across empty rooms. "Often I hear footsteps when I'm home alone," he said. "The dog pricks up her ears and runs to look—she hears them too—but we don't see anything.

Sylvia Brown, while investigating the house, saw clairvoyantly a whole mosaic of spirits. First there was a man in a long black coat with a top hat who paced back and forth. Could that have been Broderick?

Then Sylvia described black people hiding in the cellar. "They were hidden there for their own protection, but many of them were frightened and unhappy, uncertain of the future," she explained.

SAN FRANCISCO

Considering the state of San Francisco politics in the 1850s, this seems highly probable. Surely Haskell, an anti-slavery crony of Broderick's, would have aided fugitives even to the extent of hiding them if necessary in his home.

Those turbulent times have left their imprint on the pretty two-story house where many dramatic events have taken place over the years.

Of course it's haunted.

Quarters Three, the historic Haskell House is located at Fort Mason at the foot of Franklin Street in San Francisco.

THE SAN FRANCISCO ART INSTITUTE

Can unfulfilled longings trigger a ghost into being?

A group of prominent psychics hold frustrated creativity to blame for a series of hauntings that have mystified faculty and students at the San Francisco Art Institute.

The Institute is a splendid example of the Spanish Colonial revival architecture popular during the 1920s. The walls are stripped concrete dyed a soft adobe ocre, the roofs red tile. A bell tower rises above the patio in the manner of an early mission.

"There's something strange about the bell tower," students began to whisper almost immediately after the Institute opened its doors on January 15, 1927. But it was twenty years before anything really happened.

Artist Bill Morehouse is now a professor in the art department at Sonoma State College, but in 1947 he was a night watchman and student at the Institute. To reduce expenses, he decided to sleep in the tower.

He vividly recalls his first night there.. "It was around midnight and I had gone to bed on the third level. I heard the doors opening and closing down below. I'd locked them myself, but I assumed that it was the janitor, so I didn't bother to investigate. I listened to the footsteps climbing to the first level, then to the second and finally to the third.

The door knob turned and the door to my room opened and closed as though someone had entered. It was a large room and well lighted. Inside was a water tank, my bedroll and me. I saw no one but heard footsteps passing through the room, turning, then walking back to the door. The knob turned, the door opened and closed and the footsteps continued up to the observation platform."

SAN FRANCISCO

That was Morehouse's first encounter with the Art Institute Ghost, but not his last. He tells of another night when he and five friends were partying in the tower. Their laughter came to a sudden halt at the sound of footsteps approaching. "The steps came up, up, up," he says. "Just as they reached the landing, one of us yanked the door open and yelled 'surprise!' We were the ones who were surprised—there was no one there. The steps continued on, going all the way to the top of the tower."

View from Art Institute tower.

Wally Hedrick, former long-time faculty member, said his most frightening brush with the ghost occurred one night when he was working after midnight. Suddenly, he heard all the tools go on downstairs in the sculpture studio. Hurrying down to investigate, he found no one.

Working as evening registrar during those days artist Hayward King, like many others, also began to believe in the ghost. He remembers closing the school at 10 p. m. "There was no master switch then, so we would walk all around the Institute, turning off lights as we went. Just before going out we'd turn and look back. Often we'd find that one or two lights were on again in the empty building. Of course you could say that we'd missed those lights or there was a short in the electricity. You could say a lot of things. . ."

Once King and Hedrick closed the office together after all the lights had presumably been turned off. As they shut the front door, every light in the building turned on simultaneously.

Morehouse, Hedrick and King believed their ghost to be mischievous but essentially benevolent. The unexplained manifestations that livened their evenings became less and less frequent until the ghost was almost forgotten.

Then in 1968 it returned. This time its appearance was decidedly disturbing.

As a 1.7 million dollar enlargement program began, attention was once more focused on the tower, which was being renovated as a storage facility for the Institute's Art Bank Collection. It seems that a slumbering ghost was awakened.

Several students on the night maintenance shift were convinced that the ghost was not only an evil influence on their own lives but was holding up the construction project. Three of the night crew blamed the spirit for personal disasters that included a serious motorcycle accident, an attack of polio and a tragic family situation.

Another told of studying late at night in the library with his wife. "We heard the sound of chairs being broken behind us, but no one was there," he said. The building program was delayed for many months by a series of costly mistakes and near-fatal accidents.

In response to an outbreak of incidents, a group of psychics gathered for a seance in the Institute tower. With them were several observers, myself included. Frustration was the emotion picked up by all the mediums. "So many artists with such grand designs that never got anywhere. . .so many trying to put their ideas on canvas. . .many projects uncompleted."

San Jose medium Amy Chandler told of seeing a "lost graveyard," a fact later verified by the Institute historian. A cemetery adjacent to the Institute had been obliterated by early 20th Century construction.

SAN FRANCISCO

A series of pictures taken that evening by Nick Nocerino revealed the tower room not as it was but as it had been—with a door and windows that no longer exist. Others taken by Chuck Pelton showed a strange displacement of people within the room—a kind of musical chairs effect. Seance participants were photographed in motion, some fading in and out entirely. In reality none of us moved from our chairs during the two-hour session.

What that means, only the ghost can explain.

Photograph by Chuck Pelton.

The San Francisco Art Institute is located at 800 Chestnut Street.

THE MONTANDON TOWNHOUSE

"I lay a curse upon you and upon this house; I do not forget and I do not forgive; remember that!"

Can evil, angry words carry a power of their own? Is fact truly stranger than fiction?

Pat Montandon certainly has reason to think so. After reading her book, *The Intruders*, one finds it difficult to disagree.

During the 1960s the dazzling blond achieved recognition in San Francisco as hostess of a popular TV show. She gained national fame when listed by *Esquire Magazine* as one of the top hostesses in the country. The image, sustained by many flashbulbs and much newsprint, was "glamorous jet set queen." Here was a woman who seemingly had everything.

Unfortunately "everything" included a haunted house on Lombard Street.

It all began with a party, one more gala star-studded event in a glittering chain. This gathering—in keeping with the astrological renaissance of the late sixties—had a zodiac theme. An added attraction was a Tarot card reader.

The warm, festive mood turned to chill when the seer, piqued by an imagined slight, suddenly turned on Pat and snarled, "I lay a curse upon you. . ."

The words returned to haunt her in the years that followed, fearful years that found the golden butterfly ensnared in a web of dark malevolence. Her house was repeatedly vandalized and fire-ravaged. Her car was smashed several times, her career disrupted, her reputation threatened by ugly accusations, her romances blighted.

SAN FRANCISCO

Locked windows within the house opened of their own accord. A biting chill defied the normally functioning heating system and totally destroyed the warm ambience of the luxury townhouse. Two close friends who shared the house committed suicide. Repeated threats on Pat's own life forced her to hire round-the-clock guards but they could not protect her from the evil atmosphere that seemed to pervade her very being.

"I don't believe that the Tarot reader caused these things," she has emphasized. "But possibly something in that ugly incident triggered evil forces already hovering about me or about the house itself—once the scene of public hangings.

"Such thoughts would have been inconceivable to me a few years ago," she admits, "but today it would be impossible *not* to believe."

Certainly the most tragic of the circumstances surrounding Pat's residence on crooked Lombard Street was the death of her closest friend and secretary in one of the most mysterious fires ever investigated by the San Francisco Fire Department.

On June 20, 1969 a blaze unaccountably started in the master bedroom where Mary Louise Ward—who was discovered dead in bed after the fire—had been sleeping in Pat's absence. Firemen had difficulty entering the house for the front door was chained and barred from the inside. The possibility that Mary Louise had accidentally started the fire while smoking in bed was ruled out. She didn't smoke. That a guest might have been responsible also seemed unlikely, for the bedroom door was also *locked from the inside.*

Though an autopsy revealed that the victim was dead before the fire, the actual cause of her death was *not* determined. There was no evidence of heart failure, sedation or drunkenness. Mary Louise's internal organs were in good condition and she had not suffocated. The investigation was finally dropped, the cause of death remaining a mystery.

Pat moved from the besieged townhouse but continued to be haunted by the experience. Concerned for the safety of the new tenants, she enlisted the aid of two mediums, Gerri Patton and Nick Nocerino. At her bequest, the two psychic investigators visited the house.

Though Nocerino knew nothing of its history, he was able to pick up psychically not only Pat's traumatic experiences, but also those of previous tenants unknown to her. His impressions were specific, including names and details. Research on Pat's part revealed that the former residents had indeed been involved in a series of tragic events that resulted in divorce, great personal loss and/or suicide.

The strangest incident connected with the investigation involved photographs taken by Nocerino inside the house. These revealed weird light configurations, despite the *absence* of artificial lights (light bulbs, flash bulbs, chandeliers or cut glass, etc.) with their capacity for reflection. Some prints clearly show a woman bending over a drawer with one hand raised as though in surprise at some discovery. The

Photograph by Nick Nocerino.

SAN FRANCISCO

image was not on the negative and there was no one in the room at the time except Nocerino who was taking the pictures.

In an effort to verify the authenticity of the prints, Montandon arranged to have the negatives printed again under laboratory conditions with five independent witnesses present. The freshness of the chemicals was determined, negatives were brushed with a static free brush, the time of the exposure was recorded and every step of the development process observed by all. Shapes appeared on the prints that were not on the negative and several looked as though light was coming from some unknown source. The same ghostly face and figure of a woman was again clearly visible although no such person had been seen or intentionally photographed in the house. Since the whole roll had been shot there, there seemed no possibility of a double exposure.

Hoping to avert more tragedy, Nocerino performed an exorcism on the house. "It was difficult to bring myself to give validity to such an act," Montandon admitted to me, "and yet, I no longer feel uneasy about the place. Everything now appears to be stable and normal."

One can only hope.

The house, a private residence is located on San Francisco's "crooked Lombard Street."

THE HAUNTING OF ALCATRAZ

For thousands of years Alcatraz was a barren sandstone rock inhabited only by seabirds. In fact, that's how it got its name. Juan Manuel de Ayala, the Spanish explorer who charted San Francisco Bay in 1775 called the place "La Isla de los Alcatraces," (the Island of the Pelicans).

Alcatraz Island. Photograph by A. May.

Virtually escape-proof, Alcatraz was ideally suited to be a prison and became a military one in 1859. Among the very first prisoners were American Indians brought in chains and shackles — the survivors of military campaigns against the few remaining native holdouts in the far west. What a terrifying experience it must have been for them, for the Miwok Indians had long considered the island a haven for evil spirits.

Recalcitrant—or unlucky—soldiers were also sentenced to Alcatraz beginning in 1907. Their task was to chip rock to build roadways and buildings. The soil needed for foundations and landscaping wa brought from nearby Angel Island as vegetation on Alcatraz was almost nonexistent. By 1912 the army prisoners had completed the largest reinforced concrete structure in the world. Ironically, the first confined there were the inmates who built it.

SAN FRANCISCO

The Army transferred Alcatraz to the newly formed Federal Bureau of Prisons in 1933. The following year the government decided that a "super prison" was needed to house the likes of Al Capone, Alvin "Creepy" Karpis, "Machine Gun" Kelly and Robert "Birdman" Stroud. "The Rock" seemed the perfect place to isolate the most troublesome convicts. Surrounded by the cold, swift currents of San Francisco Bay, the natural isolation of the island was reinforced with barbed wire, guard towers and double-barred windows.

Additions were made to the existing prison and then—secretly—a train was sent to each maximum security penitentiary in the country. Without any advance warning — so that word couldn't possibly leak to friends who might arrange an escape—the incorrigibles were loaded on board. The train then headed to San Francisco where it rolled onto a barge headed for Alcatraz.

Alcatraz cell.   Photograph by A. May.

Once landed, the celebrity prisoners were marched up the hill to their waiting cells. For a convict like Al Capone who'd actually occupied a luxury suite in Atlanta Penitentiary it must have been a nightmare, but for anyone it was "hard time." Prisoners were surrounded by steel and concrete, their lives dominated by rules and routine. Inmates spent from 16 to 23 hours a day in their individual 5-foot by 9-foot cells.

From the dining room they could look out at San Francisco's world famous skyline. Often they watched sleek ocean liners glide off to exotic ports. All about them were constant reminders of what they were missing. At night in their cells when the wind was right, the convicts could hear the sound of revelers at the St. Francis Yacht Club only a few miles away. Often they were taunted by women's laughter and each New Year's Eve, they listened while the yachtsmen welcomed in the new year.

Failure to abide by the rules meant confinement in "D" Block, the treatment unit. Here the men were kept in their cells 24 hours a day, seven days a week, leaving only once in seven days for a ten minute shower. Offenders who did not respond were then placed in the "hole," one of four steel boxes where they remained in total darkness.

Suicides and murders were common on the Rock and an escape attempt in May 1946 ended in a bloody riot and siege that cost the lives of three inmates. Though thought to be "escape-proof," there was one attempt which may possibly have succeeded. Three inmates — Frank Morris and two brothers, John and Clarence Anglin — spent months slowly chipping holes through the rear walls in each of their cells. Working at night, they concealed their work with false cardboard grates. The men made model heads of themselves from wire, newspaper, concrete, paint and human hair. Each night these dummy heads were placed in their beds to fool the guards during their head counts.

On June 11, 1962, the three inmates climbed up through the utility corridors and crawled through a ventilator onto the roof, then headed to the north end of the island where they slipped into the water on flotation devices they'd made themselves. The three men were never seen again.

SAN FRANCISCO

Though most believed that they were drowned in the icy waters of the bay, no one really knows. At any rate, they may well have found death more desirable than life on Alcatraz Island.

On March 21, 1963, Attorney General Robert Kennedy officially closed the prison.   Expensive to maintain — one guard was required for every three inmates — and deteriorating rapidly from the salt air, the penitentiary no longer seemed practical to maintain.

With the exception of a caretaker, the island remained empty until November 20, 1969.   Then, in the early hours before dawn, ninety American Indians quietly boarded two private pleasure boats moored along the Sausalito waterfront and sailed the five miles to Alcatraz. The group —college students, some married couples and several children aged two to six—called themselves "Indians of All Tribes."   Their purpose was to stake a claim to the island which they believed was theirs by virtue of a forgotten treaty which offered unused government land to Native Americans. They hoped to establish a cultural, educational and spiritual center on the island.

But very soon the Indians discovered the same problem that had caused Kennedy to close the prison. Alcatraz has no natural resources. Everything needed on the island, from water to wood, had to be ferried across the bay.   It was a tedious and expensive process.

At first where was much excitement and encouragement. The Indian "invasion" generated publicity. Celebrities such as Jane Fonda, Anthony Quinn, Merv Griffin and Jonathan Winters made trips to the island. Troops of Boy and Girl Scouts sent toys, the United Auto Workers donated a generator.   Federal officials sat around cross-legged on blankets laid out in the crumbling cell blocks discussing the social needs of the Indians.

Then twelve-year-old Yvonne Oakes, daughter of one of the activists fell from the the third floor of a cellblock stairwell and was killed.   The rest of the Oakes family left the island and never returned.   It was the beginning of the end.

The grounds at Alcatraz. Photograph by A. May.

Despite prohibitions enforced by the tribal council, alcohol and drugs were smuggled onto the island. On the night of June 1, 1970 a massive fire illuminated the foggy skies over Alcatraz. Four buildings, including the warden's mansion and the historic lighthouse built in 1854 , were destroyed. Federal officials blamed the Indians, Indians blamed government saboteurs. By now most of the original Indians settlers had left. The rest had begun to fight among themselves.

The end finally came on June 11, 1971 when twenty federal marshals descended on the remaining Indians—six men, four women and five children. They were searched for weapons and taken to Treasure Island under protective custody. The occupation of Alcatraz was officially over.

* * *

Today the island is maintained by the Golden Gate National Recreation Area. Each year more than 900,000 visitors tour the crumbling remains of "the Rock."

SAN FRANCISCO

Some of them see ghosts.

Not surprisingly, much of the phenomena occurs around areas associated with the penitentiary's worst tragedies.   One of them is the Block C utility corridor where inmates were killed during the 1946 uprising. A National Park Service watchman reported a strange "clanging" noise coming from the empty corridor which stopped as he opened the door. When he closed the door it began again.

Other employees tell of ghostly voices coming from the hospital wards where maimed and crazed prisoners were frequently confined; and screams, running footsteps and crashing sounds have been heard on Cell Blocks A and B.

The single eeriest spot is said to be Cell 14-D, one of the infamous "holes". It's always cold in 14-D, even when the temperature elsewhere rises to the 70s. Rangers feel an "intensity" in the cell, an emotion strongest in the corner where naked, broken inmates once huddled.

One of the most tragic stories regarding the cell centers around Rufe McCain who was kept in this tiny steel box for three years and two months as a punishment for attempting to escape. Eleven days after being released, McCain stabbed another convict to death.   When tried for murder, McCain was acquitted when the jury ruled that the living hell of 14-D had destroyed him—body, mind and spirit.

On September 5, 1984, Rex Norman, a ranger spending a lonely night on the island, was awakened by the sound of a heavy door swinging back and forth in Cell Block C.   Upon investigation, Norman could find nothing to account for the disturbance. When the sounds continued on subsequent nights, the park system decided to bring Sylvia Brown into the case.

On September 10, the psychic accompanied by a CBS-TV news team, began her investigation. One of the first areas toured was the prison hospital. As Sylvia was about to enter one of the rooms, she paused in the doorway. "I don't understand this but I see all kinds of cards and notes tacked up on the wall. They're everywhere."

Norman was at her side in an instant, "Do you see anything else?

Sylvia shook her head in bewilderment. "Only the letter S. All I see is an S. I don't know what it means."

Norman was excited. "It could be S for Stroud," he suggested. "Robert Stroud—the famous 'Birdman'—spent ten and a half years in the hospital, in this very room. People think he had birds in his cell, but that isn't true. He just studied birds. He had hundreds of notes and cards tacked up all around him—things he was learning about birds."

Sylvia turned, moving down the hallway, then entered another room. "Oh, I feel such panic here, such anguish. It's awful, it's almost unbearable.   There's something else. . .it's so cold, it's so terribly cold in here."

Norman nodded. "This used to be the therapy room," he explained. "the most violently psychotic prisoners were brought here to be bathed in ice water and wrapped in icy sheets. It seemed to have a calming effect on some of them. Afterwards they would go to sleep."

Sylvia, progressing on to the prison laundry room, had another strong reaction. "There was violence here. I see a man. He's tall, bald, and has tiny little eyes. I'm getting the initial M, but I think they call him 'Butcher.'"

Norman was puzzled. "It could be, I just don't know." But Leon Thompson, an ex-convict who had done time at Alcatraz and had been invited to join them, moved forward and stood beside Sylvia. "I remember a man we used to call Butcher. His name was Malkowitz, Abie Maldowitz, but we called him Butcher. He'd been a hit man with Murder Incorporated before they caught him. Another prisoner killed him right here in the laundry room."

Sylvia felt a wave of pity for the spirit of this prisoner, who, for some

SAN FRANCISCO

A cell unit of Alcatraz.   Photograph by A. May.

unaccountable reason, had chosen to remain in prison even though death had freed him. She decided to hold a seance in the penitentiary dining room; and soon her spirit guide, Francine, was speaking through her.

"What's happening?" Thompson asked eagerly. "Do you see him? Do you see Butcher? What's he doing?"

"He's walking toward us. He's standing now on the other side of our table watching us," Francine, the spirit guide — speaking through Sylvia — explained.   The guide, spoke now to the spectre before her, "You don't have to be afraid of us. No one wants to hurt you," she reassured him.

"What does he say?" the others wanted to know.

"He says, 'I've heard *that* before.' " Now she addressed Butcher once again: "When I leave this mortal vehicle known as Sylvia Brown, I will return to the other side. Come with me, follow me into the light. You will be much happier there. You will find people who will care for you, people who want to help you."

"What does he say?" Thompson wanted to know.

Francine sighed. "He doesn't believe me. He's going to stay here."

And apparently he has, for the rangers who look after the abandoned prison continue to report eerie disturbances late at night. The prospect of the Butcher's seemingly eternal sentence to the lonely penitentiary continues to prey on Sylvia's mind. She hopes to be allowed to return once again to perform yet another seance.

Boats to Alcatraz Island depart several times a day from 9:45 a. m. to 2:45 p. m. from Fisherman's Wharf in San Francisco. Reservations are advised. Telephone: (415) 546-9400.

SAN FRANCISCO

THE MANSIONS HOTEL & RESTAURANT

There was a saying in the 1880s that though a man might make his fortune in the desert, he came to San Francisco to spend it. Richard Craig Chambers was a classic example. The wealth that built the mansion at 2220 Sacramento Street in 1887 had its source in a Utah silver mine. After many failures, he had become one of the richest and most politically powerful men of his time.

A key figure in the development and settlement of the American West, Chambers' life was a saga of migration, struggle, repeated business reverses and finally discovery of a bonanza. At eighteen he'd left his home in Richland County, Ohio and set off across plains and mountains. Reaching Sacramento at the height of the gold rush, he left immediately for the Morman Island diggings on the American River. By 1851, he'd moved to the Upper Feather River Mines in Plumas County, then pushed on to Nevada migrating with the mining frontier as it penetrated the continent eastward from California.

Chambers explored the entire west traveling as far north as Helena, Montana, before settling in the Utah Territory where he became superintendent of Senator George Hearst's Webster and Bully Boy mines. In 1872, the chance discovery of a rich vein of silver proved the turning point of his life, the culmination of more than twenty years of struggle. Immediately setting to work to raise development capital, Chambers assembled a prominent group of backers that included Senator Hearst. A deal was struck, Chambers emerged part owner and superintendent of the mine. The official name was the Ontario, but many called it the "Plumas Asylum". Chambers, remembering his lean days, always managed to find jobs for his less fortunate comrades.

With money, he made money and that money bought power. Chambers founded a newspaper, becoming one of the most powerful political voices in the inter-mountain region. It wasn't enough. San Francisco beckoned. The Sacramento Street showplace he built was a statement. Next came admittance to the Pacific Union Club in 1892. By 1894, he was listed in *Our Society Blue Book.*

Chambers died in 1901; his wife had preceded him. Since the couple had no children, two nieces inherited the mansion. They soon turned the classic revival structure into two houses by moving the original building to the east side of the lot and adding a second half with its own entrance and address. Perhaps the women didn't get along. Maybe the hobby of one, Claudia Chambers, had something to do with it. Claudia adored pigs and raised them as pets.

Then something bizarre and terrible happened. Claudia was killed in a freak accident. The legend has it that she was sawed in half. Today, no one can quite agree how it occurred. A series of people lived in the double house after that, but no one stayed long. Once the pride of Pacific Heights, the place had degenerated into a run down rooming house when

Bob Pritikin at the Mansions Hotel.
Photograph by Vern Appleby.

Bob Pritikin bought it in 1977. A kind of miracle man cut from the same cloth as Chambers, Pritikin, an advertising genius, is the author of *Christ Was An Ad Man* and *Pritikin's Testament.* Transforming the delapidated relic into an elegant hotel and restaurant was the ultimate challenge.

A true Renaissance man, Pritikin harnessed all his talents—interior designer, magician, art collector, musician and recording artist (piano and musical saw!) — to pull it off. The Victorian mansions were not so much converted as embellished. Rooms were decorated in crushed velvet, brocade, crystal and pigs — ceramic pigs, wooden pigs, metal pigs and painted pigs. The new owner was determined to keep Claudia happy. Though one can only wonder at her reaction to the dinner show,

The Mansions Hotel.   Photograph by Vern Appleby.

which includes renditions of "Moonlight Sawnata" and "The Last Time I Sawed Paris", performed by Pritikin on his saw, or to the magic tricks involving a floating head--said to be a likeness of her.

Is it any surprise the two Mansions are said to be haunted? An obstreperous guest was decked by a heavy door that suddenly came loose from its hinges and fell on him, a toilet seat lid ripped itself loose from steel hinges, a crystal wine glass exploded in the presence of several guests and the diaphanous form of a lady has been seen frequently on the grand staircase.

To determine what exactly was going on, Pritikin called in psychic, Sylvia Brown. "There's a girl here. Her name is Rachel and she's dressed in a turn of the century maid's uniform," Brown told him. "Sometimes people feel her presence. It's like someone brushing against cobwebs. Rachel died at nineteen and remains frozen at that age. It was a traumatic death. She planned to be married but contracted tuberculosis. It came on suddenly. Now she's confused and wonders why so many people are invading her world."

Lorraine and Ed Warren, the demonologists who exorcised spirits from the "Amityville Horror," visited the Mansions recently and felt a heavy concentration of energy in the opulent Josephine Room. "There's an extremely heavy presence here," Lorraine said, "but it isn't negative."

Recently I spent an evening at the Mansions with a group of psychic researchers. We set up our Ouija Board in the Josephine Room and found the spirits extremely responsive to questions of a personal nature. As we were about to quit, the planchette board became extremely agitated, whirling about almost out of control. Identifying itself as J-U-L-I-A, a presence asked that we help her son, Henry Ross, by sending him light. Henry, she explained had committed suicide in the house when he was only twenty-one.

Just then a waiter, who'd appeared to remind us that it was past midnight, pointed out that the branches of a large potted palm tree were moving briskly. No air currents seemed responsible for the phenomenon.

Most certainly the building did go through some sad times, but they seem far removed from the present day ambience. If ghosts can be "cheered up," this is the place for it. Surely no one could feel gloomy there for long. A blithe spirit like Bob Pritikin with his moonshine and magic has a penchant for making things happen. What ghost could resist such a "lively" atmosphere?

The Mansions Hotel and Restaurant is located at 2220 Sacramento Street, San Francisco, CA 94115. Telephone: (415) 929-9444.

SAN FRANCISCO

It not just what we inherit from
our mothers and fathers that haunts us.
It's all kinds of old defunct theories...beliefs
...I've only to pick up a newspaper and
I seem to see ghosts gliding between the lines.

—Henrik Ibsen

SAN FRANCISCO BAY AREA &
THE EAST BAY

THE RENGSTORFF HOUSE

THE PENINSULA SCHOOL

THE ATHERTON HOUSE

THE WHEELER OFFICE

BLACK DIAMOND REGIONAL PRESERVE

KOHL MANSION

THE RENGSTORFF HOUSE

Rising in eerie silence amid the lonely marshlands east of Mountain View is the Rengstorff mansion. The ornate structure — a montage of Gothic and Victorian architecture complete with widow's walk and classical columns — has stood vacant since the mid-1960s, a ghostly reminder of a colorful past.

The old house, now vandalized and dilapidated, was built in 1887 by Henry Rengstorff, a German immigrant who amassed a fortune farming and shipping grain, and became one of the founding fathers of Mountain View. Six children were born and grew up there in apparent happy prosperity. In 1906, Rengstorff, who had arrived in this country with only four dollars in his pocket, died in the house—a very wealthy man.

Shortly afterward, Perry Askam, the Rengstorff's orphaned grandson, came to live at the family house. Askam grew up to be a successful Broadway singing star, appearing in many popular musicals. In 1945 he and his wife returned to the Rengstorff home. Once again the place was a social mecca. Between concert appearances with the San Francisco Symphony Orchestra, the Askams entertained lavishly. The gala era ended with Askam's death in 1961.

The house was then acquired by the Newhall Development Company and a series of disputes began. Should the place be demolished, relocated or refurbished? For nearly twenty years historians, developers and city politicians have hotly debated the issue, while within the house itself a different sort of energy has made itself felt.

A series of tenants and neighbors reported unexplainable manifestations—the sound of crying late at night, lights that flashed on and off, uncanny cold drafts. During the many vacant periods, passersby have reported seeing a young woman with long hair standing in the upstairs window staring out at the marshland below.

Thr Rengstorff House prior to restoration. Photograph by C.J. Marrow.

During the early 1960s Max and Mayetta Crump lived in the house. Crump was at that time manager of the Newhall Land and Farming Co., and part of his pay included the right to live in the Rengstorff mansion. For a time the Crumps and their two young sons lived uneventfully in the house, then they began to hear thumping noises on the stairs. Crump bought fly paper which he placed on the steps. Though they continued to hear noises, the fly paper was undisturbed.

During the night Mr. and Mrs. Crump would be awakened by a child crying, but upon investigation they would find their children sound asleep. They decided to move the whole family into one room at night, but the sounds of crying in other parts of the house continued.

Crump then borrowed a rifle specially sighted for night use. Night after night he sat up watching for whatever might appear. Nothing ever did though the noises continued.

During their three year tenancy, the Crumps eliminated the possibility of an animal in the house, for the fly paper was never disturbed nor were there any other traces found. The theory of a human practical joker was also discarded.

"Finally I just came to believe that there was something in the house that I couldn't understand," Crump admitted in later years to Robert I. Pack who was investigating the house for the *Times-Tribune*.

Though the Crumps grew accustomed to their unseen housemates, friends did not. Once a couple dropped by when the Crumps were out. While the husband was standing before the front door, the knob turned. His wife could see into the house from a large window at the side.

It was empty.

Adding to the mystery was a set of restraining cuffs which were among the furnishings within the house when the Crumps moved in. No one knows what part they may have played in the long history of the old mansion.

The time came when no one would live in the house. Once a showplace, the windows were boarded up. Whether this was to keep the living out or the dead in nobody was quite certain. What to do with the vacant, frequently vandalized home, was debated. Numerous schemes were formulated over the years. Among those involved were the three young men convicted of the Chowchilla school bus kidnapping. They had planned to use some of the ransom money to acquire and renovate the house.

In an effort to find out what was behind the strange happenings, medium Sylvia Brown held a seance in the house. Almost immediately she was confronted by the apparition of a hawk-faced man being pushed in a makeshift wheelchair. One leg had been severed in a farming accident, the other crippled by arthritis. He was bitter, angry. . .

But that wasn't all. Soon a more horrific scene appeared. It was the strangling of another man in an upstairs bedroom. Someone had stolen up behind him with a bell cord. "They want his money, the family wants his money," she explained, "everybody's fighting about money."

Sylvia's experience differs from the original family version, but then *something* must account for the ominous energy that dominates the house.

The Rengstorff House has been moved to Shoreline Park in Mountain View where it has undergone a total renovation to the tune of $1.5 million. Every effort has been made to duplicate the original decor. The mansion is open to the public for free tours from 11 a.m. until 5 p.m. On Tuesday, Wednesday and Sunday it may be rented for special occasions.

Interior view of Rengstorff House prior to restoration. Photograph by C.J. Marrow.

Telephone: (415) 903-6073

THE PENINSULA SCHOOL

A bride dead under mysterious circumstances. A grand mansion built at great cost and then abandoned.

The legend begins here and then twists and turns into a dark labyrinth of possibilities. The impressive structure built by San Mateo Country Assemblyman James Coleman in 1880 cost $100,000—a fantastic sum in those days. According to one nostalgic story it was to be a gift for his lovely wife, the former Carmelita Nuttall, a woman described by contemporary newspapers as "peerless in beauty and accomplishments."

The mansion was nearing completion when a tragic event occurred that cast a somber shadow over the place for more than a hundred years. Coleman returned from a business trip to the San Francisco hotel suite that he shared with Carmelita. Though it was 5 a. m., the dutiful young wife rose from bed and proceeded to unpack his bags. Somehow, as she was removing a gun from his valise, Carmelita accidentally shot herself.

It's said that the distraught bridegroom never set foot in the Peninsula palace that had only just been completed. The house changed hands several times over the years, no one lingering long. In 1906, a young woman is said to have ended her life there, hurling herself headlong down a steep stairway.

When the founders of the Peninsula School purchased the mansion in 1925, they acquired a resident ghost as well. Almost from the beginning, Carmelita Coleman was a loved (and feared) member of the school community. The romantic tradition of her tenancy has grown with the years, sparked by some very vivid experiences.

Yesterday's Victorian elegance has been replaced by today's space age funk but the legend of Carmelita is still very real. For more than fifty years there have been stories of shimmering lights, unexplained footsteps and pets that refused to enter the building. Generations of children have told of glimpsing the wraithlike figure of a woman dressed in green. Some say the woman herself is green. Once an entire class saw the apparition.

Peninsula School.   Photograph by C.J. Marrow.

Ken Coale, a former caretaker, remembers quite vividly being awakened at 3 a. m. one summer morning by the sound of footsteps. "I had been sleeping on a couch in the staff room," he recalls. "The footsteps seemed to come from the room just above me on the second floor.   I lay there absolutely petrified." Finally Coale forced himself to track the sounds. They grew louder and louder as he climbed the stairs.

Then just as he reached the landing a door opened before him. He entered and the door closed behind him. The room from which the footsteps had seemingly come was empty. The only window was closed. Opening it, Coale looked down. It was a forty foot drop to the ground below and there was no indication of anyone having taken that exit. The house was quiet now. Whoever or whatever had been there was gone.

Mary Anne Collins, a parent of a former Peninsula student and a one-time custodian, felt Carmelita's presence many times but never actually saw her.

A spirit photo taken October 31, 1982—Halloween night.

Joe Starr and Monique Caine, former teachers at Peninsula, tell of an overnight at the school when some twenty children saw an apparition. Starr described the vision as a green woman who appeared to be transparent. As he attempted to approach the figure it moved backward but remained visible for a full five minutes. Starr asked the children to sketch what they had seen and found that all the drawings were similar—a green woman who seemed to shimmer.

Starr encountered the apparition another night. This time the green lady confronted him in a black hallway when he was all alone. He flipped the light switch, but nothing happened. Man and ghost stared at one another for a few very long moments. Then the vision simply disappeared.

Many of the students are quite blasé about their ghost. "I see it all the time," Shawn Kelman told an interviewer. "She's green." Panos Koutsoyannis told of "running through it"—to the amazement of a group of playmates.

Barney Young, former director of the school, believes the ghost to be a benevolent one, pointing out that no one has ever been hurt by it. "The green lady has a way of taking hold of us. Kids may start out by being rather skeptical. 'I don't believe in that kind of stuff,' a newcomer will say. I always think to myself, 'Just ask him about the ghost in another year, after he's been here at night some time. That's enough to make a believer of anyone.' Often kids will say, 'Come quick! There's the ghost!'

Teachers think they're being put on until they see it too."

Anna Mary Peck, who researched the Peninsula School for a study in folklore in 1973, found mystical significance in the very greenness of the ghost. In ancient heraldry, green symbolized eternal life, youth and hope —very appropriate for an old school ghost.

A decorator's nightmare, but a child's delight, the Peninsula School was the site of the movie, *Escape from Witch Mountain.* If houses can be typecast—this one was a natural.

At last a seance was held at the school. In the presence of some fifty people, a voice speaking through the San Francisco medium Macelle Brown introduced herself as the original owner; and related a heretofore untold tale of an unhappy marriage, a lover, a very jealous husband and a murder—her own.

Then, to everyone's surprise, another ghost "came through" claiming to be Carmelita's father, R.R. Nuttall, but dismissing her story as "hogwash."

"Why shouldn't I be here?" he demanded to know. "It was my money that built the place, not Coleman's." Nuttall then explained that he visits the school from time to time to note the modern improvements and watch the students. He enjoys children, likes progress, has no messages and wishes no one ill.

What really happened?

How will we ever know when even the ghosts themselves can't get their stories straight.

The Peninsula School is located at Peninsula Way in Menlo Park. Telephone: (415) 325-1584

THE ATHERTON HOUSE

Who rules the roost at the historic Atherton house? The domineering matriarch? The ineffectual son? The rebellious daughter-in-law? Or the mysterious cat lady?

Can the battle of the sexes transcend the grave?

Consider the cast of characters. First there's Dominga de Goni Atherton who built the house — now a historical landmark — in 1881. During the lifetime of her millionaire husband, Faxon Dean Atherton, she was condemned by convention to a subservient role. While Faxon spent most of his time tomcatting around San Francisco, she did the family homework — managing their country estate. The town of Atherton evolved from their holdings.

The Atherton House. Photograph by C.J. Marrow.

Immediately after Faxon's death, Dominga bade a hasty farewell to suburbia and established permanent residence in San Francisco. Construction of an impressive mansion at 1990 California was, in a sense, her declaration of independence.

Then there was Gertrude Atherton, Dominga's audacious daughter-in-law who shocked the haughty Athertons by writing racy novels. And, finally, there was George who barely had the initiative to tie his own shoelaces.

During the 1880s, Dominga financed George in a series of financial ventures that invariably failed. Then one evening in 1887, the California Street house was the scene of a grand ball honoring visiting Chilean naval officers. "It was a brilliant affair, one for which the new house was admirably suited," Gertrude wrote in her memoirs.

"There were dowagers with acres of whitewashed flesh. . .bulging above corsets. . .hips as large as their bustles; girls in voluminous tulle, all looked me over disapprovingly."

That was because Gertrude had disdained the traditional ball gown, wearing instead a devastating creation of white cashmere which she described as "fitting every part of me like a glove."

Gertrude enjoyed the disapproval of the good ladies of San Francisco, but George did not enjoy *her* disapproval—Gertrude had called him a "mere male, nothing more"—and at the height of the party, he impulsively accepted the Chilean guests' invitation to accompany them back home.

The following day when George showed signs of changing his mind, Gertrude outmaneuvered him. She was not about to allow a few Georgeless months to slip through her fingers. Cleverly she goaded, "If you have any pride, you will stay here in San Francisco and make something of yourself."

He left.

Gertrude got more freedom than she bargained for. After a few nights at sea, George died of a kidney attack. The captain decided that the San Francisco scion should be shipped home for burial. Hoping to preserve him, the resourceful Chileans placed the body in a barrel of rum and continued on to Tahiti where another captain agreed to take George back to San Francisco. According to legend, the family first learned of his demise when the cask was delivered to 1990 California, where an unsuspecting butler uncrated his pickled master.

"I had an uneasy feeling that George would haunt me if he could,"

S.F. BAY AREA & THE EAST BAY

Gertrude admitted.   She didn't linger in the area, literally taking her inheritance and running.

The mansion had a quick succession of owners.   Then in 1923, Carrie Rousseau remodeled the place into separate apartments, selecting for herself the thirteenth unit—formerly the orchestra chamber of the grand ballroom. Sharing an adjoining apartment — once the banquet hall — were her fifty cats.

Carrie died in 1974 at ninety-three, attended by her feline companions. Human tenants knew little of her but had plenty to say about the spectral inhabitants of the house.   Singer Aurora Booth, when interviewed by San Francisco Chronicle reporter Kevin Wallace, described a rushing wind that roared through her tiny apartment.   Jerrie Landewig, a dental assistant, complained of a rapping on her bedroom door just as she was dropping off to sleep, and told of a former tenant who was frightened out of his tower apartment by filmy apparitions.

These witnesses, who have since moved from the house, were quite certain that George was the spirit causing the excitement. But at a seance, medium Sylvia Brown picked up on three female spirits. "They just don't like men," she warned the two new owners—both men.

Unaware of the house's history, Sylvia began to pick up psychic impressions of the apparitions which appeared before her. "One keeps saying, 'This is my dwelling.' She seems awfully possessive," Sylvia said. "She's short, very buxom and highly volatile, a lot of energy there." (Dominga Atherton weighed two hundred pounds and was five feet tall. A native of Chile, she possessed a fiery Latin disposition.)

The next apparition was described as an attractive blond with "very definite likes and dislikes, very independent for her time. She wanted to be liberated and was." (An apt description of Gertrude, if her own writings are to be believed.)

The third apparition, subordinate to the others, was identified as "Carrie."

Hot and cold running spirits made the evening memorable. Room temperatures changed frequently and drastically, keeping the eleven of us who participated in the seance busy putting on and taking off our jackets and sweaters.

Photographs taken that night by Nick Nocerino reveal a series of spectral "blobs" that seem to float about the house. Tape recorders picked up a strange moaning sound that no

Spirit photograph at the Atherton house.   Photograph by Nick Nocerino.

one heard during the seance, but did not pick up the sound of a tinkling bell—the type used to summon servants— which was clearly heard by all.

"There is a male spirit here," Sylvia said at last, "but he's so pale and frail. There's nothing to fear from him. " Then she cautioned, "But bad vibes could come from female ghosts who want things done their way and won't tolerate much male interference."

Does feminism transcend the grave? Sylvia Brown believes that it does and suggests that the Atherton mansion would make a dandy women's resource center.

The Atherton Mansion, once again a private residence, is located at 1900 California, on the corner of Octavia and California Streets, in San Francisco.

S.F. BAY AREA & THE EAST BAY

THE WHEELER OFFICE

Webster defines the poltergeist as "a mischievous ghost held to be responsible for unexplained noises."

This prosaic definition hardly describes the pandemonium that has terrorized homeowners, theater goers, patrons of bars, hotels, bakeries and even used car lots. It doesn't mention the variety of smells that have pleased or sickened witnesses and can't begin to convey the horror of finding oneself choked by unseen hands or the sight of sudden bursts of flame, flying knives or falling stones.

Students of the phenomena have attempted to explain poltergeists in one of three ways: earthbound spirits, energy caused by suppressed frustrations, or the devil.

It was a very bad day at the office for members of George H. Wheeler's court reporting firm, who finally gave up the business as usual pretense on June 16, 1964 and called police to their office on Franklin Street in Oakland. It was fervently hoped by all that the long arm of the law could reach into the realm of the supernatural.

After several weeks of bedlam that defied explanation, they had come to believe that their otherwise ordinary office had been targeted by poltergeist forces. Whether earthbound spirits, suppressed frustrations or the devil—they wanted **OUT**.

What happened still remains a mystery to those involved, but Dr. Arthur Hastings, a University of California parapsychologist, developed some very provocative theories.

When asked to investigate the case, he soon discovered a strange set of circumstances. Early in January a twenty-year-old man had been employed by the firm as a typist. He was apparently liked by all, but treated somewhat as a child. "There's no doubt that he was low man on the totem pole and knew it," Hastings explained to me.

"A few weeks later phones began to ring for no reason. Once answered, there was no one on the line. The ringing would then begin again so quickly that there was no time for an outside prankster to dial, wait for an answer, hang up and dial again," Hastings says. "This began in February. By March the calls had increased so that it became impossible for anyone to call the office because the lines were constantly busy, yet no one was calling out.

"Every telephone had to be replaced, although the phone company was positive that each was in perfect working order. Once this had been accomplished, the mysterious calls stopped."

Unfortunately this was only the beginning. All at once typewriter springs began to break. As fast as Joseph Morrow, the typewriter repairman, would fix one machine, another would suddenly break. Mystified, Morrow could find no cause for such an occurrence. The machines were mostly new, had always been serviced regularly and until that time had worked perfectly.

James Ambrosia, the city electrical building inspector, was called and gave the office a thorough going over. He could find nothing wrong—electrically speaking.

Next, coffee cups began to blow up and bulky six-foot cabinets tipped over for no apparent reason. Framed plaques and pictures flew off the wall and a ceramic vase shot seven feet from a closet shelf across the room before crashing to the floor.

By this time everyone in the office was certain that the young employee was the culprit, for the disturbances invariably occurred in his presence. At the same time, they were all in agreement that he was doing nothing manually to cause them.

Another strong indication of his guilt became apparent when the young man would leave the office, located on the third floor of a large building, to visit acquaintances on other floors. The phenomena went with him,

S.F. BAY AREA & THE EAST BAY

occurring everywhere he went. Meanwhile back in the court reporting office, peace and quiet prevailed.

"Surprisingly, there was very little animosity directed toward the man," Hastings says. "Though all agreed that he was causing the problems that were literally destroying the office and most accepted the theory of pent up hostilities somehow triggering the violence, they remained tolerant. It was as though they, themselves, somehow assumed a portion of the responsibility. It was a kind of family situation with all the implicit characteristics of conflict, punishment and forgiveness inherent in such a relationship."

The young man was allowed to take his typing home. Immediately the troubles stopped. When he returned, they began again. The pattern continued until the inevitable publicity brought the police into the case.

"After hours of questioning, the man confessed and was released almost immediately," Hastings says. "No one — probably not even the police—took the confession seriously. To have tipped over a large filing cabinet in the presence of six people without their awareness would have been difficult in the extreme. Yet somehow the arrest and public atonement satisfied some need. Though his job remained open to him, the young man insisted upon quitting. He has not been heard from again. It is unlikely that he will be.

What could he possibly do for an encore?

Franklin St., Oakland CA

BLACK DIAMOND MINES REGIONAL PRESERVES

A pair of lovers got a thrill they hadn't bargained for when they stopped to park by the Rose Hill graveyard south of Pittsburgh.

The isolated little coal miners' cemetery in the Black Diamond Mines Regional Preserve seemed ideally suited to total privacy. But the romance cooled to chills when they looked up and saw a "glowing lady" gliding above the headstones in their direction. The woman cowered under the dashboard while the man fled down the hillside, finally stumbling ignominiously into a stream.

The apparition faded, but not the stories about the area. The lonely, windswept burial ground is flanked by the remains of two ghost towns, Nortonville and Somersville, to which—during the heyday of the Black Diamond Mine—hundreds of men and boys came from Wales hoping for a brighter future in the golden land. Their excitement was brief, their dreams short lived; for the coal proved of poor quality and the mine petered out.

Little remains of the once bustling era but the cemetery guarded by five stately cypress trees rising sentinel-like against the amber hillside. Many of the pioneers, including Noah Norton, are buried there, a silent testimony to mine disasters and black lung, of women who died in childbirth and children lost to smallpox and typhoid.

Unfortunately they have not been allowed to rest in peace. Graves have been excavated by looters and gravestones — some lettered in Welsh — have been stolen.

According to psychic Nick Nocerino, this wanton desecration is what has caused the eerie phenomena that surround the graveyard where ghostly laughter, cries and the tolling of bells have frequently been reported.

S. F. BAY AREA & THE EAST BAY

Nocerino has visited the cemetery late at night, making contact with the spirits who have voiced their displeasure. In a newspaper article, he urged that the tombstones be returned. Some were dumped unceremoniously on his front yard late at night. The stones were returned to the cemetery, but many are still missing. Though more than 100 known grave sites have been exorcised, disturbances continue.

Spirit energy photographed at night above Rose Hill Cemetery by Nick Nocerino.

Perhaps the living may still make amends to the angry dead. Peace may be returned to these unhappy spirits when their property—mute testimony to their mortal existence—is finally restored.

To reach the graveyard, take Highway 4 out of Concord east to the Loveridge Road exit, head south, then turn left at Buchanan. Turn right on Somersville and drive to the end at the preserve's parking lot where the trail to Rose Hill Cemetery begins.

THE KOHL MANSION

None doubted that it was a fatal attraction, the dangerous liaison of its day.

Whatever leading citizens said publicly, most certainly their private view was that the upstairs, downstairs relationship between the married socialite, Frederick Kohl, and his mother's maid, Adele Verge, had clearly gone too far.

Born in 1863, Frederick Kohl, son of the Alaska Commercial Company shipping magnate, grew up on the Kohl estate, now Central Park in San Mateo. Young "Freddie" hunted with the hounds and rode polo ponies on the Peninsula, site of the elegant summer estates then popular with wealthy San Franciscans. At his father's death in 1893, he inherited a multi-million dollar estate. Dashing Freddie was considered a catch. His choice was the lovely Elizabeth "Bessie" Goody, an aristocratic Washingtonian renowned for her singing talent as well as her beauty.

It was a marriage made in heaven—at least that's what the bridegroom said, and who could doubt him. In 1909, the couple sailed to Europe with Kohl's mother who, while there, engaged a French maid, Adele Verge. Green-eyed, raven haired, Adele was high strung, almost haughty. She came with the highest recommendations from the very finest families.

Problems developed months later on another family vacation, this one to the Glenwood Inn in Riverside. While there, the high handed Adele got into an argument with a chauffeur and not only slapped him but spat in his face. Fred Miller, manager of the Inn, had her arrested. "She belongs in an asylum," he told the police. The court disagreed. Adele was a bit on the temperamental side, but surely not deranged. She went free.

Kohl discharged her and suggested a return to France, offering to pay her way. Refusing, Adele followed the family north. In San Francisco,

S.F. BAY AREA & THE EAST BAY

she filed suit against both her former employer and Miller charging malicious arrest and harassment.

On the afternoon of June 8, 1911, Adele Verge — according to newspaper accounts--listened, "an unnatural glare in her hard and blazing eyes," as the judge ruled against her. She would receive nothing.

Rushing from the room, Adele was waiting by the elevator when Kohl emerged on the first floor. Drawing a derringer from her handbag, she fired point blank at him. "I knew it would come to this," he muttered as he slumped to the floor. Adele turned and fled, but was apprehended while walking aimlessly along Market Street. "I don't know why I did it," the former maid sobbed to a French Catholic priest with whom she spent the night praying for Kohl's recovery.

Kohl lived, but the bullet, lodged dangerously close to his heart, remained imbedded there for the rest of his life. When the victim refused to press charges, no trial was held and the would-be murderess was deported to France and confined to an asylum.

Seemingly, Bessie and Frederick put their troubles behind them. The following year they began work on an elaborate Tudor style mansion on 40 acres of land in Burlingame, then a small, conservative town with one doctor, newly paved streets and a streetcar that climbed Hillside Drive, ending just one block from the estate. On Christmas 1914, the Kohls opened the manor doors for their first party and continued to entertain lavishly for two years. The rosebrick mansion towered over an estate that included a tennis court, greenhouses, a rose garden, a large carriage house and a 150,000 gallon reservoir. The mansion alone cost $424,000. All this was not quite enough, it would seem, to dispel memories of Adele.

In 1916, the couple separated. Freddie suspected Bessie of seeing other men. She took her singing talents to Europe, entertaining World War I troops and Kohl consoled himself with the glamorous Marion Louderback Lord. Whatever happiness they found was shortlived, the bullet in his chest was a constant source of pain; and, as though that weren't enough, Kohl began to suffer debilitating anxiety. His troubles with Adele were far from over. Upon her release from the asylum, she'd written him threatening to finish the job.

In 1920, Adele wrote first from Quebec, then British Columbia—she was coming closer and closer. Kohl's attorneys urged the Canadian authorities to arrest Adele and have her extradited to California to face trial. She was arrested, but extradition refused. Released at last, Adele disappeared. Kohl, certain that she was on her way to kill him, fled with Marion to Del Monte Lodge in Monterey.

On November 23, 1921, he breakfasted alone in his suite. At 10 a.m. a single shot was heard. Kohl was found, still seated at the table, a .38 caliber revolver clutched in his hand. The bullet had passed through his skull, lodging in the wall.

One way or another, it appeared that Adele Verge had gotten her revenge.

But was this the end of Freddie? Hardly. The story had barely begun. The Kohl estate was bequeathed to Marion Lord, who rented it to United Artists for production of the the most ambitious movie of the era, *Little Lord Fauntleroy.* The film capped the career of "America's Sweetheart," Mary Pickford, who played both Fauntleroy and his mother. You either liked Pickford or you didn't. Those who didn't must have been thrown into diabetic comas from the abundance of so much unadulterated sweetness.

Nevertheless, the effect did manage to change the image of the Kohl mansion. Pickford in her black velvet suit, lacy white collar and shoulder length curls did much to dispel both the rumors of the ill fated affair and the reality of the scandalous Marion Lord.

The Sisters of Mercy now considered it appropriate for a nunnery. The 63- room mansion was acquired by the order, which totally transformed it. Theirs was a regulated life. Novices abstained from unnecessary conversation and were warned to guard against familiarity with anyone.

They were never to raise their eyes immodestly. Visits to town were forbidden. Tradition had it that if a girl took even a single step off the grounds she would have to begin her novitiate anew.

The Kohl Mansion. Photograph by Vern Appleby

It's difficult to imagine that such behavior would adversely impact outsiders, but incredibly it did. Beginning in 1924, members of the Ku Klux Klan, in their guise of protectors of "truth and justice," began to terrorize the sisters. There were letters and phone calls which culminated one night in 1925 with the arrival of white hooded thugs who drove their cars, horns honking, around and around the convent before setting a 40 foot cross ablaze on a nearby hill.

As though threatened violence from without wasn't bad enough, the women gradually became aware of a mysterious presence within the mansion. One of the novices slept in a fourth floor dormitory room. Often she awakened to find a white powder in such "strange places" as the sisters' shoes, on the stairs, and on the tops of drapes which were twenty feet above the floor. Sisters sat up all night hoping to apprehend the intruder, all to no avail. There were footsteps, unaccountable footsteps — and that was all.

Visitors sleeping in the third floor guest room reported hearing the sound of invisible gravel thrown at the window.   Then there were limping footsteps coming from Freddie's billiard room down the long corridor.   Freddie had had a limp, someone recalled.   But Freddie was dead.

At first the nuns suspected a few high spirited girls of playing upon the superstitions of the others, but after some persistent interrogation this theory was abandoned.   The spirits involved were of a different and seemingly far more dangerous derivation.   Exorcism seemed the only solution.

Priests were called in to liberate the convent from the mysterious force that seemingly permeated the place.   Two masses were said.   The fathers led a procession of fifty nuns, blessing every room and closet in the house and sprinkling holy water throughout the gardens.   Did it work? Apparently not, for in 1931 the nunnery was closed.

Freddie's a stubborn case, it seems.   The visions, the eerie sounds in the night still persist.   Present day staff members complain about the elevator that goes up and down by itself and a professional who came in to clean up after a particularly rowdy Halloween party felt the house "vibrate" for hours.

But now it would appear that Freddie has undergone a personality change.   Perhaps not the happiest of men in life — surely not the luckiest—today he appears in his element.   The Kohl Mansion has evolved into a private high school, concert and reception hall with Freddie assuming a kind of public relations role.   No longer the guilty, anxiety ridden victim of an unfortunate association, the "new" Freddie is something of a social butterfly and patron of the arts.   Considering the lively interest sparked by his long ago legend and present day antics, Freddie is one ghost who is very much a social asset.

S.F BAY AREA & THE EAST BAY

The Kohl Mansion is located at 2750 Adeline Drive, Burlingame, CA 94010. Telephone (415) 343-3631.

While yet a boy I sought for ghosts,
   ...with fearful steps pursuing
Hopes of high talk with the departed dead.

— Percy Bysshe Shelley

PENINSULA & MONTEREY COASTAL AREAS

THE MOSS BEACH DISTILLERY

THE RED, WHITE AND BLUE BEACH

THE STEVENSON HOUSE

BINDEL'S RESTAURANT

SUNSHINE VILLA

BROOKDALE LODGE

THE MOSS BEACH DISTILLERY

Who is the mysterious "Blue Lady" who returns to haunt the cliffside restaurant, her high heels echoing a phantom Charleston eerily into the night?

Some whisper that she's the unfortunate Virginia Rappe who died during a party hosted by Roscoe "Fatty" Arbuckle, the legendary silent film star, in his St. Francis Hotel suite.

Calling the affair an "unhallowed orgy," the unscrupulous district attorney saw to it that Arbuckle was tried and condemned in the press, then prosecuted him not one time but three in one of the most sensational cases in San Francisco history.

Virginia was described as a model, a starlet and a few other things. The murder weapon was said to have been a coke bottle. Others speculated that Arbuckle crushed her with his own weight. The first two trials resulted in a hung jury, the third gained Arbuckle an outright acquittal. It was a hollow victory. His career ruined, the former comedian died a broken man a few years later.

But what about Virginia? Many believe the pretty party girl returns in spirit to the speakeasy built on the site of another ill-fated watering hole that burned down a few years before.

The Moss Beach Distillery, originally a hotel-cum-whorehouse built in 1927—some six years after Virginia's death—was constructed on a steep cliff overlooking the sea during an era when the Half Moon Bay area was notorious as San Francisco's biggest supplier of illegal liquor from Canada. The abundance of secluded beaches and coves along th isolated stretch of rugged ocean was an open invitation to rum runners. Bootlegging was dangerous business, murder and hijacking common. But that didn't stop film stars and politicians from flocking there.

Virginia Rappe was remembered as being one of the liveliest. It's easy to imagine her drawn to the scene of earlier revelries, mischievously startling staff and patrons for more than sixty years.

Others suggest a Dashiell Hammett heroine as the legend's source. His girl with silver eyes wore a glistening blue gown and frequented a coastal roadhouse. Surely something or someone delights in opening and closing the creaky ladies room door and dancing a lively Charleston in seemingly empty rooms.

The Moss Beach Distillery, June 1990.

Medium Sylvia Brown recently conducted a seance at the request of NBC TV's *Unsolved Mysteries* series. During the course of the evening, Brown made contact with a melancholy shade who identified herself as Mary Ellen Moreley. It seemed that Mary Ellen had died nearby in an automobile accident. Her last thoughts were of her three-year old son. She lamented leaving him motherless and now — unaware of the passage of time — comes back to seek him. A check of old newspapers reveals the death of a Mary Ellen Morely, the victim of a car crash, which occurred close to the area.

PENINSULA & MONTEREY COASTAL AREAS

Yet many insist the ghost is yet another habitue of the speakeasy. This candidate loved two things; the color blue and the piano player. The second love proved her undoing for the pianist was the jealous sort who didn't take kindly to her flirtations with the clientele. One night he stabbed her to death in a jealous rage on the beach below the restaurant.

Over the years chefs, waitresses and patrons have not only heard the ghost, but seen her. Managers working late at night would hear all the faucets suddenly come on. They'd go to shut them off and return to find their office locked from the inside. Once a young boy ran screaming from the restroom where he'd been confronted by a woman in blue — covered with blood. Another night an out of towner stopped at the restaurant and asked the bartender, "Who was murdered here? I feel very strong vibrations over there," she explained, pointing to the spot where the piano once stood.

An even stranger tale was reported by Sheriff's Deputy Jim Belding who attended an impromptu seance with several employees at the restaurant. There was an inexplicable cold spot and a candle that suddenly ignited—but no apparition.

Belding and his partner left the restaurant at 3:30 a. m. and headed north on Highway 92. Then suddenly Belding's car developed a mind of its own — swerving first to the right and then to the left. A blazing white light appeared before them. Belding swerved once again, smashing the car. Miraculously they survived the crash and went off in search of help. When they returned a tow truck was already on the scene.

Later, when Belding went to pick up his car, the tow truck driver inquired about "the lady." When Belding looked blank, the mechanic persisted, "The pretty girl in the short blue dress, kind of like a costume. She was standing in the road crying and bleeding."

The deputy just shook his head.

The Moss Beach Distillery is located on the corner of Beach and Ocean streets in Moss Beach. Telephone: (415) 728-5595.

THE RED, WHITE and BLUE BEACH

A woman with a reputation for ghost chasing can expect to be asked anything. But most frequently, it's "Have you ever seen one?"

The answer is "no." I haven't seen ghosts, but I've surely felt their presence. One even accosted me at the nude beach in Santa Cruz.

It was the scariest night of my life.

It began on another, far pleasanter evening. At a crowded Tahoe restaurant, a friend and I shared a table with another couple, Bill and Vivian Marraccino. The usual get-acquainted question, "What do you do?" led to surprises for everyone.

"Have I got a ghost for you!" Bill exclaimed when I told him that I was a writer specializing in psychic phenomena.

"There's this haunted house down in Santa Cruz—all kinds of stuff happens there. Things fly around the room, lights go on and off. . ."

"Tell her about the ghost," Vivian broke in. "It's an old sailor who walks out the back door of the house and strolls about the camp grounds. He looks so picturesque in his old rain slicker and cap that a new guy—Jim Hilburn, an engineer—tried to photograph him. Jim got quite close to what he thought was a flesh and blood, if a bit eccentric man. Then, as he focused his camera, the old sailor faded away."

"Then there's the window," Bill picked up the narrative, "the window that doesn't exist." He explained that they and other campers at the Red, White and Blue Beach have often observed a lighted window on the hill above the water. "It really surprised me the first time," he recalls. "I couldn't remember any buildings in that area. I thought it was just a barren hillside with nothing on it.

PENINSULA & MONTEREY COASTAL AREAS

"The next day I discovered that it *was* just a barren hillside with nothing on it."

Of course I had to investigate this one for myself. A few days later I drove to Santa Cruz intending to interview Ralph and Kathy Edwards, the owners of the house and camp grounds. Even on a sunny day the place looks like a setting for a Gothic horror story. The Coast Highway winds its way through deserted stretches of hills and sea. On a weekday in November there was very little traffic.

The nudists can't complain of peeping toms here, I noted, turning off the road at the red, white and blue mailbox. Nothing else marked the narrow offroad which could easily be missed by passing motorists.

The narrow road wound downward from the highway, twisting and turning around rolling, mound-like hills. As I approached the isolated farmhouse, I felt that I had stepped back in time a hundred years. If ever a house looked haunted, this one did. The tall, two-story structure was like some lonely sentinel, a mute survivor. Of what, I wondered: penetrating fog and sea gales certainly. But what else?

Ralph Edwards met me at the gate. He was a tall, rangy man with a taciturn manner. "I hear you have a ghost," I ventured.

"Better talk to my wife."

"You mean you never saw it?"

"I didn't say that." He turned back to his gardening.

Kathy Edwards proved the opposite of her laconic husband. She was full of stories—all of them frightening. "Things are relatively quiet now—those footsteps, they aren't much. They happen so often, Ralph wouldn't get any rest at night if he ran downstairs to check every time we heard them. And the doors slamming by themselves, that's nothing. They do it most every day. My perfume bottles dance around a lot and we hear the sound of crystal shattering but never find anything broken.

"But when the girls were living at home, that's when the house was *really* active. My daughters used to have a terrible time at night. Something seemed determined to shake them right out of their beds. Sometimes they'd make up beds on the floor thinking to get away from it, but there

The Edwards home at the Red, White and Blue beach.

was no escape. Every time they'd pull up the covers something would yank them away. I remember Ronda was working as a medical secretary—a really demanding job that kept her very busy. Sometimes I'd hear her pleading with the bed to let her sleep.

"My son, Roger, didn't believe his sisters, so one night he slept in Ronda's bed. Nothing happened and he was soon asleep. Then in the middle of the night he was awakened by what he thought was an earthquake. The bed was shaking so violently that it seemed to leap right off the floor.

"Since the girls married and moved away, whatever it is seems to have shifted its attention to the first floor. People just won't stay over night in this house. We had our last guest several years ago. A young relative

PENINSULA & MONTEREY COASTAL AREAS

sleeping on the couch was awakened by a rooster crowing. He could see its outline perched on the arm of the couch at his feet. But when he turned on the light nothing was there."

The Edwardses have never kept chickens.

Kathy tells of a Navy picture of Ralph's which was hanging in the living room. One night it flew off the wall and sailed five feet before crashing to the ground with a force so great that some of the glass splinters are still imbedded in the wood. The nail that had secured the picture remains in the wall.

"If you think any of this is funny, don't laugh too loud," Kathy advised. "I told a visitor about our ghost once and he laughed at me. That skepticism didn't amuse whatever lives here one bit. Suddenly a drawer opened by itself and a baby shoe flew out and hit him on the side of the head. That stopped his laughing in a hurry.

On Thanksgiving Day of 1975, Kathy Edwards had just opened the refrigerator door when a large plant left its standard and flew toward her—a distance of some twelve feet. Her daughter prevented a serious injury by grasping the heavy pot in mid air. But the mess could not be avoided. The plant and dirt that had been in the pot crashed against Kathy and splattered the inside of the refrigerator.

Ronda was the target of another attack which occurred one evening with nine people present. A glass of wine sitting on the piano flew through the air and deliberately poured itself down the front of Ronda's decollete dress.

"We have our own theories about that one," Kathy says. "Perhaps the ghost was jealous. In life she may have been very flat chested—Ronda definitely is not."

One mystery that continues to plague Kathy is the window on the hill originally described by the Marraccinos. "I kept hearing about it. Then one evening I had to deliver a telephone message to the beach. As I walked back, I looked up and saw this great cathedral-like window on the side of the hill.   It was very clear and I could see someone walking back and forth behind it.

"Something seemed to draw me toward the window, yet at the same time I felt that if I went there I'd never come back.   I forced myself to return to the house.   The next day I tramped all over the hill looking for some sign of what it might be, but found nothing.   I never saw it again."

A few weeks later I returned to the house accompanied by a research team that included a group of mediums .   The psychics walked about the house and grounds noting their impressions.   I was the only one in the party who knew anything of the background of the place and I had not discussed it with anyone.

Chuck Pelton was the first of the mediums to speak.   "There's a lot of current in the house, a lot of energy.   Lights go on and off here by themselves."

"That's for sure!" Edwards affirmed.   "The campers are always asking about those blinking lights.   They say, 'Don't you and Kathy ever go to bed?'   Actually the lights go on by themselves long after we've turned everything off and gone to sleep."

Chuck continued, "I see an old man wearing a raincoat and hat.   I feel dampness, rain, mist.   I think he was a sea captain."

This, of course, was corroborated by Kathy, who added that she'd found an old rain slicker and cap hanging on a hook on the back porch when they'd moved into the house.   "At least a dozen people a year tell me they've seen an old man in a raincoat.   I wonder sometimes if it couldn't be the sea captain who built this house in 1857."

The talking stopped.   We were aware of the sound of animals howling outside.   It was dark now and nothing could be seen from the windows. Chuck Pelton and Nick Nocerino went outside to investigate.

PENINSULA & MONTEREY COASTAL AREAS

Sylvia Brown, director of the Nirvana Foundation, began to speak, "You feel a heaviness in your chest at night, don't you, Ralph?"

"Yes," he nodded.

She continued. "Things move around in this house. They seem to get lost, disappear for no apparent reason."

"They sure do," Kathy agreed. "The first year we lived here we were ready for the divorce court. I thought he'd taken things; he thought I had. Now I know that neither of us had. It was someone else, some*thing* else. Once I had a letter to deliver for one of the campers. It disappeared right out of my hand and appeared a day later in a laundry bag."

"I see an older man," Sylvia said. "He's wearing a long coat and walks about the grounds. In his life he killed an intruder. He doesn't like company even now. The people who lived here before were an angry, unhappy family. There was a lot of hatred, a lot of unresolved problems. I see unhappy young people ... a beautiful girl ... blood. There was a stabbing here. A baby died here, too. There were evil acts committed in the past."

Nick and Chuck had returned and I was very glad to see them. The atmosphere of the house had grown heavy and oppressive. I had a sense of danger, an emotion that I'd rarely experienced in the other houses investigated over the years. A dog was whining softly, cowering under a chair.

Nick Nocerino, a lifelong medium, sat down beside me. His words were anything but comforting. "There has been evil in this house—murder and incest. I see an angry man who dominated his children. They were virtual prisoners here."

Kathy recalled that the former owner, a woman in her nineties, was the last of a large family who had lived for decades in the isolated farmhouse. "The stories she told me of her life were sad," Kathy said.

"Her father took all the children out of school and refused to allow their friends to visit. He forced his children to work long hours in his dairy and then, as his health failed, he made them wait on him hand and foot. She seemed very bitter."

Nick went on, "There's been smuggling here—people mostly. People were brought here and some of them never left. They're buried here. There was bootlegging too."

"Yes," Edwards agreed, "we found bottles of homemade whiskey and the remains of a still."

"A young girl came to visit about the turn of the century. Her name was Gwendolyn. She was murdered."

Kathy gasped. "A girl named Gwendolyn *did* disappear mysteriously while visiting her uncle, who owned the place. That was in the very early 1900s. No one ever heard from her again. But a couple of years ago Ralph and I decided to put in a barbecue pit and dug up a skeleton. Thinking that we might have tapped into an old Indian burial ground, we called in an expert from UC Santa Cruz. He said the bones were those of a woman buried eighty to ninety years ago."

The number of amazing "hits" says a good deal for mediumship, but did little to allay my fears. Directly across from where I sat in the living room was a window facing onto the front yard. From time to time I saw streaks and blobs of light at the window. It's my imagination, I told myself.

I could live with that until Ethel Pelton who was sitting on the floor opposite me and directly under the window, spoke in a tight, choked voice. "I feel something terrible behind me. Something's going on outside. I know it is and I'm scared."

It really didn't help to have my skeptical friend, John Wilson, a Menlo Park attorney, confide that he too felt a sense of dread and oppression.

It was nearly midnight as the seance broke up.   John and I walked out into the black night.   A thick fog was creeping in from the sea.   I felt certain that the evil presence menacing the Edwards house had attached itself to me.   Sick with terror, I stood shivering in the damp sea air—uncertain whether to continue on in the dark or go back into the afflicted house.

John made the decision for me.   "Come on, let's get out of this place," he said, grasping my arm and pulling me toward the car.   Just as we got in a great dark bird appeared out of nowhere and hovered above us.   As we slowly navigated the narrow dirt road to the highway, the ugly creature preceded us.   It had a wingspan of some six feet.   What was it, I wondered—an owl, an eagle?   I recalled the place had at one time been known as the Eagle Run Dairy.   What a relief when this gruesome harbinger of doom finally faded away in the night.

But that was not the end of our troubles.   A heavy wind seemed to come up out of nowhere as we crossed the Santa Cruz mountains, making it difficult to keep the car on the road.   I began to see flashes of light like bolts of lightning and blobs of white energy.   There seemed no doubt that some evil presence was pursuing us.

Some of that apprehension dissipated in the familiar atmosphere of my apartment.   The streaks were gone, the blobs were gone, yet I could not rid myself of the feeling that I wasn't alone.   Many times in the days that followed, I glanced up from my typewriter, certain that someone was looking over my shoulder.

Had I picked up a spectral hitchhiker?   I recalled the story of "Lu," a woman who had visited the farmhouse with her boyfriend, a long time friend of the Edwardses.   Lu had felt so uncomfortable in the house that she'd left almost immediately.   At home, she experienced a sense of possession.   Again and again she heard the words, *unfinished* and *unburied*.   She saw a vision of a man and large searing white spots.

Slowly as the days passed, the sense of being watched diminished.   I was alone again — really alone — and very glad of it.   It was all imagination,

I decided, and was beginning to believe it. And then one evening Nick called.

It seemed that he and Chuck had photographed the house while outdoors investigating the howling sounds. "What did you get, werewolves?" I tried to sound flippant.

"No, just blobs and streaks of light," he answered, also trying to sound flippant.

The pictures had been taken in darkness and yet the house was clearly revealed. The upstairs window of a darkened bedroom was illuminated and above the living room — where the seance had taken place — were round blobs of light and sometimes lightning-like bolts.

Spirit photograph by Nocerino/Pelton team.

Some nights I wonder what they're doing down at the nude beach—but so far, I haven't had nerve enough to go back and find out.

The Red, White and Blue Beach is located on Highway 1 six miles north of Santa Cruz — look for the red, white and blue mailbox on the seaside of the road.

PENINSULA & MONTEREY COASTAL AREAS

THE STEVENSON HOUSE

"Who is that woman in black?" the tourists sometimes ask, pausing in the doorway of the charming nursery.

Barbara Burdick, curator of the Stevenson House, a museum in the Monterey State Park, is at a loss to answer the question. The "who" remains a mystery. The "what" is for certain.

The woman in black is a ghost.

Legends are legion concerning the former boarding house now named for its most illustrious lodger, Robert Louis Stevenson. Many speculate that the "lady in black" is actually Fanny Osbourne—the alluring woman Stevenson came all the way from Scotland to woo and subsequently married.

But most—including Barbara Burdick—believe the ghost is Manuela Giradin, owner of the house during Stevenson's stay. They think the spirit of Manuela is in fact reliving the last tragic weeks of her life.

During the summer of 1879, Mrs. Girardin lost her husband, Juan, in a typhoid epidemic. Then in early December her two grandchildren fell ill of the same disease. Manuela worked desperately to save the children, tending them literally night and day. Then the devoted grandmother caught the fever from her young patients. She died on December 21st, never knowing that her grandchildren had recovered largely through her efforts.

Over the years a variety of phenomena have been observed, almost invariably during the first three weeks of December. "People from out of state who know nothing of the legend will see all kinds of things," the curator says. "A rocking chair in the nursery will suddenly begin to rock of its own accord, or they'll smell carbolic acid—often a sickroom disinfectant.

"Each year an apparition is seen. 'Isn't it nice that the housekeeper is in costume just like you?' someone will say, pointing at what appears to be a blank wall. Perhaps I wouldn't believe—not all the park employees do—if I hadn't seen her myself."

The haunted nusery in the Robert Louis Stevenson house.
Photograph by C.J. Marrow

Late one foggy afternoon when Barbara Burdick was preparing to lock up, she noticed a woman in black gazing intently down at the children's bed. "She was oddly dressed in a long gown with a high lace collar, but aside from that looked as 'lively' as anyone," she recalls.

"Despite the stories, it never occurred to me that she wasn't just another tourist. When I explained that it was closing time, she nodded understandingly.

"I turned to leave and then looked back, wondering just how she had managed to get inside the barred room. The nursery was empty."

The Stevenson House, located at 530 Houston St., is open every day but Wednesday from 10 to 11 a. m. and 1 to 4 p. m. Visitors must register for tours in advance. Telephone: (408) 649-2836.

PENINSULA & MONTEREY COASTAL AREAS

BINDEL'S RESTAURANT
now known as SUPREMO

Can love transcend the grave?

Jehanne Powers thought so. The widow of Gallatin Powers, founder of the world famous restaurant, Gallatin's, Jehanne bravely continued its management until her own death. Today the newly refurbished restaurant is known as Bindel's.

Built in 1838, the historic Stokes Adobe was once a grand mansion, the residence of James Stokes, first mayor of Monterey. Today it's an elegantly appointed dining house filled with valuable antiques.

The polished silver candelabra and exquisitely cut glass chandeliers recall a time when Monterey was the Spanish capital of California. Surely many of the appointments were in the house during the exciting days when the city was menaced by the dreaded pirate, Hippolyte de Bouchard. Others date from the tempestuous era when Monterey was besieged by American forces. Could it be an energy implant, some psychic remnant of a bygone terror, that continues to "haunt" the restaurant today?

Kara Caswell, Jehanne's former partner, feels otherwise. "There were two kinds of things happening when I was there," she explains. "One kind involved ghosts that people saw, the other involved things that happened. Maybe ghosts also caused the happenings — they definitely appeared to be directed by some kind of intelligence.

"Why am I so sure? Because most of the time the victims seemed chosen for a reason. We'd discover that a certain employee hadn't been quite honest. Before we could fire him, he'd quit. The stories were always the same. 'Something' seemed to be shaking him, pushing him down the stairs, or he'd hear footsteps following him about the place late at night when he knew he was all alone. It seemed like a force was literally trying to shake these people up, telling them to shape up or get out— and that's exactly what happened.

"Once we had a bartender who was cranky. He fixed drinks well enough, but customers just didn't like him. It's hard to fire someone on the basis of personality alone, but that seemed the only course to take.

Supremo Mexican Restaurant & Steaqueria, formerly Bindel's Restaurant.

We didn't have to worry long. He complained about glasses falling off the bar, but no one paid much attention. Then one night I heard him yell. Rushing into the banquet room, I saw that the whole back bar — a massive mahogany thing — had begun to move. For a minute I thought we were having an earthquake, but everything else was still. Not so much as a single prism of crystal from the chandelier was moving. That was the last we saw of that bartender. He left immediately."

Jehanne Powers believed that something was trying to attract her attention as well. One night she and Kara had closed the empty restaurant at 3 a.m. only to have the Muzak turn itself on full force as they reached the parking lot.

Many windows opened by themselves and often every light in the place turned on—with no master switch. One night the police called Jehanne to report a light inside the restaurant and asked her to meet them there with a key so they wouldn't have to break in. Driving there, she vividly recalled having turned every light off. Jehanne found the restaurant surrounded by police. One man took the key and went inside.

As he stood in the entry, the policeman heard the sound of steps climbing the stairs, crossing the banquet room and entering a small room off to the side. Following, he approached the open door and demanded, "Come out with your hands up!" Suddenly the door slammed shut knocking the gun out of his hand. At last, joined by reinforcements, he tore open the door. The tiny room—which has no window or exit--was completely empty.

On another evening Kara's son, Charles, was polishing silver in the banquet room when he was startled by the sound of someone crying. Looking up, he saw the figure of a young woman in a long white dress. "I'm so sad," she said, wringing her hands.

Jehanne believed this to be the ghost of Evangeline Estrada whose sweetheart, Juan Escaba, was killed in the brief war for statehood. "It's easy to imagine that the grieving girl might remain at the scene of her romance, waiting endlessly for her lover to return," she speculated.

Again and again diners inquire about the lady in black. "Are you having a costume party upstairs?" a man asked, explaining that he'd glimpsed an older woman in a long black gown ascending the stairs. There was no costume party.

Another man felt a gown sweep the back of his chair. Turning to see if there was room for her to pass, he looked directly into the face of an older woman who seemed to melt into nothingness as she reached the stairway.

This time Jehanne believed they were seeing the ghost of Hattie Gragg, a very strong-willed woman who had lived in the house prior to her suicide in 1948. The Graggs were a proud family who had fallen on hard times. It was a tragedy for her heirs to have to sell the historic house but it was heavily mortgaged. Jehanne felt that Hattie bitterly resented seeing strangers — restaurant guests — in her home.

But Hattie Gragg's animosity toward the restaurant—and possibly herself—was not the only problem facing Jehanne Powers. "I think my husband is here too," she confided to me. "Ours was a very close, extremely loving relationship. I think he wants me with him on the other side."

Were Jehanne's suspicions correct? One can only speculate. At the time of the interview, her health was failing. She died and Gallatin's passed into the hands of another restaurant owner. The venture was not a success. The building remained closed and shuttered for five years. Then in March 1991 it reopened under new management and with a new name, Bindel's. Today the restaurant is know as Supremo.

And the ghost? The present owner and staff are certain that *something's* there — something nice. "Yes, we all feel a presence," Darryl Brewer, the manager, says, "but it's a welcoming one. Our guests feel it too. Perhaps all the lovers are united, all scores settled. Whatever's there, we're sure it likes us."

Supremo (formerly Bindel's) is located at 500 Hartnell Street, Monterey, CA.

Telephone: (408) 373-3737.

PENINSULA & MONTEREY COASTAL AREAS

THE SUNSHINE VILLA

The crumbling Victorian loomed eerie and abandoned atop Beach Hill for nearly a decade.

Everybody has stories about the old McCray hotel. Alfred Hitchcock once lived nearby and the McCray was said to have been the inspiration for the building in his film, *Psycho.* Herbert Mullins, who killed thirteen people including a priest in a confessional, lived in the hotel during the height of his murderous rampage. Santa Cruz police admit that after the place was closed it was the scene of satanic rituals as well as drug dealing. Historians speculate that the building rests on the bones of angry Ohlone Indians. Many say the house — now renovated and reincarnated as a retirement home — is haunted.

The strange story may have had its beginnings hundreds, perhaps thousands, of years ago when the Ohlones climbed the hill to pay grateful homage to the sun for its daily return. Most certainly rituals were performed on the hill overlooking the sea where the sun disappeared into darkness each night.

The known history of the property has its beginnings in the mid-1860s when Dr. Francis M. Kittredge climbed the hill, admired the view and decided to build a house there for his wife.   The Kittredge home was a lovely place known for its beautiful gardens, but the owners moved on. There was an attempt to establish a residential hotel, but it failed.

Then along came James Phillip Smith, a millionaire, who purchased the building for his family home. It was Smith who gave the Sunshine Villa its name.   A man with big ideas to match his deep pockets, he turned the house into a community showplace. Surrounded by velvety green lawns and overlooking the San Lorenzo River as well as the sea, the mansion was the site of lavish teas, balls, musicals and banquets for visiting dignitaries.

The Sunshine Villa reached its apex in Santa Cruz social history when the owners sponsored the Venetian Water Carnival. The river was dammed at the Beach Hill curve to form a sparkling lagoon. Electric lights—a rarity in those days—were strung along the banks to highlight the festivities. Smith picked up the tab for everything insisting upon the very best. In an era when all was elegance, when women were lovely and men dashing, the Sunshine Villa shone.

But the Smiths moved on, a series of new owners came and went. No one remaining long. Finally the mansion was converted once again into a hotel, the McCray. A former resident and owner, Charles Kilpatrick, who lived there until he was nine and then returned in 1977 upon the death of his parents, reports seeing a ghost.

"I saw it for the first time when I was six," he told the *Santa Cruz Sentinel* in 1986. "It was a blue energy cloud that materialized suddenly, growing as big as a gorilla."

In 1987 the property was acquired by its present owners. After nearly two years of remodeling and major expansion, which involved lifting the old hotel off its foundation and moving it ten feet, the doors opened on the new Sunshine Villa. Sunshine Villa is an assisted living facility for senior citizens which includes a restaurant-sized dining room, an arts and crafts complex, a beauty salon, and a courtyard with a gazebo.

The face-lifted villa now resembles a charming confection rising from the grassy hillside. No traces of the delapidated McCray remain— except......

"The place is haunted," according to Yevona Thomas, the housekeeper. "I was leaning over cleaning the pool table and something cold came over me, pushing me."

Stacy Smith, a health and wellness coordinator, also reports a chilling experience. "I felt this cold presence. It was like a whisper on my neck, kind of a gentle kiss in a way. Turning, I could see nothing; but I definitely felt a presence close by."

Bonnie Sousa, who used to work nights at the Villa, recalls hearing the sound of a young woman's voice calling from the ducts of the gas fireplace used for central heating and seeing blue lights in the blackened hallway.

Jan Kertz, a Watsonville psychic, called in to investigate the house, sensed tragedy. "There was mental illness in the old McCray. It got so heavy that even the drug addicts were uncomfortable there. A woman was murdered in the hotel but it was covered up somehow. She's still hanging around, hoping some one will find out about it."

The Sunshine Villa. Photograph by Vern Appleby.

Kertz attributes the phenomena to an "energy vortex" located on the site. "The Indians recognized this, but they dealt with it sacredly. We must learn to do the same."

The management of the villa feel confidant they're on the right track. Any presences that might be detected are positive, protective ones, they believe—with good reason. The reconstruction job that transformed the place was completed October 16, 1989. After months of effort, the building was finally bolted down, fully operational. The next day a massive earthquake devastated much of Santa Cruz. The Sunshine Villa sustained no damage whatsoever.

The Sunshine Villa is located at 80 Front Street, Santa Cruz, CA 95060. Telephone: (408) 459-8400.

BROOKDALE LODGE

Kim Gilbert's one of those gorgeous blondes who slink through mystery novels. Her likes spring from the the pages of Raymond Chandler, Dashiell Hammet, Mickey Spillane. Voluptuous figure, long golden hair, husky voice—she's a mystery buff's dream come true.

Kim Gilbert. Photograph by V. Appleby

But Kim isn't a figment of a writer's imagination. She's a real tell it like it is type whose father is a police lieutenant. A spunky lady, who wants to be a cop herself. She's also a free spirit who believes in spirits — at least one of them — because she's seen it herself.

In 1989, Kim's parents, Lee Ann and William Gilbert, bought the once famous Brookdale Lodge. The eight-acre property, nestled between Ben Lomond and Boulder Creek on Highway 9, includes 46 motel rooms, nine cabins, three cottages, 64 condominium units, a cafe, and retail shops as well as the lodge. Built in 1923, the lodge itself houses offices, a bar and the famous Brookdale Restaurant where an actual creek and waterfall cascade through the dining room.

During its heyday in the '20s, '30s and '40s, the Lodge was a getaway for the rich and famous. Joan Crawford, Tyrone Power, Howard Hughes, Henry Ford, Hedy Lamarr, President Herbert Hoover and Rita Hayworth were among the notables who signed the guest register—plus more than fifteen million not-so-famous tourists who came to eat in the restaurant featured in "Ripley's Believe It Or Not" and to see the property often used as a backdrop for magazine shoots and Hollywood films.

PENINSULA & MONTEREY COASTAL AREAS

Toward the end of the glitz days, some people began to stay the night on the off chance of encountering "Sarah," the niece of the lodge owner, who some fifty years ago, drowned in the creek that runs through the dining room. Then came a series of disasters. One of the original buildings burned to the ground in 1952. Five people died in the fire. There was a serious flood in 1955, then another fire. The place changed hands several times, finally standing vacant. Most recently the lodge had a reputation as a hangout for alleged drug dealers.

William Gilbert, a traffic commander and former Tenderloin District cop who served 23 years on the San Francisco police force, put an end to that in a hurry. "We have zero tolerance for drugs," William said. "We tell people when they call for reservations that the lodge is under new management and if they're into drugs, not to come."

The Gilberts asked their daughter, Kim, to manage the lodge while they undertook the task of restoring it to its former glory. She accepted the job while attending the police academy in San Jose.

Soon after arriving at the lodge with her small daughter, Kim began to hear strange tales from locals about ghosts said to walk the halls. She learned the lodge had been owned by gangsters in the '40s and that a number of people met violent deaths there. Kim wants to be a cop, right? Everybody who has ever watched a detective movie knows that police are supposed to be, if not cynical, then at least skeptical. Kim had her skeptical number down cold. Dismissing the stories as nonsense, she nodded her head with a certain wary tolerance, "Yeah, yeah, sure........"

Then the doors started slamming — for no apparent reason. The jukebox and television began to blare — on their own. Toilet paper rolls unwound unaided simultaneously from both the men and women's restrooms. Kim noticed mysterious cold spots during sweltering summer days. The scent of gardenias slowly began to waft through the lobby, down the halls, past the bar.

Morning after morning she was awakened at 3 a.m. by a voice calling her

Brookdale Lodge.   Photograph by Vern Appleby.

name. Then one night after a big band appearance she and the staff were relaxing in the lounge. It was 3 a.m. and they were about to call it a morning when all heard the sound of laughter in the conference room above. Many years before this had been a game room and there was still a pool table in the corner. They heard a cracking sound, then more laughter. Rushing upstairs Kim and the others found balls scattered all over the pool table. The room was empty.

Late one night when the lodge was locked and empty, she heard big band music coming from the Mermaid Room. Now a shadowy storeroom with no working electrical outlets, the room had once been notorious. It was a glass enclosure behind which male guests could watch women — each tagged with a number — cavort above them in a large pool. It was said they had only to make their selections known and their choice would soon be waiting in a tourist cabin across the road. A secret underground panel once connected the buildings.   Sometimes Kim could hear the sound of laughter, the clinking of glasses.

One night, while sitting in the lounge after the bar closed at 2 a.m., she was startled by the sound of a small child running in the lobby a few feet away. Kim looked through the large double fireplace shared by both rooms and saw a little girl in a dress reminiscent of the 1940s. Assuming that it was her own child playing dress up, Kim hurried into the lobby intending to reprimand the child and take her back to bed. The room was deserted. Rushing upstairs, she discovered her daughter fast asleep.

"What I had seen was a real little girl," Kim says. "She looked like any other except for the old fashioned clothes.   As I sat beside my own child's bed thinking about it, I remembered a couple who'd come to check out the lodge's wedding facilities. They'd talked of seeing a child too, a little girl that no one else saw or could account for."

That night made a believer of Kim Gilbert.   The small storeroom at the back of the lodge kitchen, a room covered with weird designs said to have been drawn by devil worshippers, was no longer a vague curiosity. Kim was afraid to go in there. Soon she noticed an unpleasant smell coming from a small dark room off the banquet hall. According to the story, mobsters had been buried there.

Kim really didn't want to investigate. Instead she called the Campbell based Church of Nova Spiritus. Two ministers arrived. Carrying lighted candles, they wandered through unfinished rooms, down dusty hallways, peering into tunnels and through iron railings, all the while praying for the eviction of any evil spirits present.

The prayers apparently had a reverse effect. "If anything, they may have annoyed the ghosts," Kim admitted later. "Shortly after the failed exorcism, I awoke one morning to find wooden planks ripped off the wall in the banquet room across from that small room where the mobsters are supposed to be buried."

Kim says ghosts per se don't bother her. She speculates, "Maybe some of them were lively, party people in life and now they simply enjoy being where the action is. My parents are trying very hard to bring back the old Brookdale Lodge feeling—the good part, the glamor and the fun. We want that kind of 'spirit,' but if the good ghosts have to leave with the bad—I'd just as soon they all go. There *is* something wrong here—I feel it."

Whatever's going on certainly hasn't affected business. If anything it's helped. "Of course," she admits, "I do get a few wacko calls. They're thinking *Exorcist* I guess — Linda Blair's head spinning around. I tell them to forget it."

A look around the newly renovated property reveals no spinning heads, no blood oozing from beneath carpets, no slime dripping from the walls. Anything but! Still, one thing's certain: Ask for spirits at the Brookdale Lodge and you may get more than a shot of whiskey.

Brookdale Lodge is located at 11570 Highway 9, Brookdale, CA, 95007. Telephone: (408) 338-6433.

PENINSULA & MONTEREY COASTAL AREAS

All that we see or seem
Is but a dream within a
dream.

–Edgar Allen Poe

SOUTH BAY & CENTRAL CALIFORNIA

THE WINCHESTER MYSTERY HOUSE

THE GHOST IN THE HAUNTED TOY STORE

PACHECO PASS

THE WINCHESTER MYSTERY HOUSE

Every night is Halloween at Sarah Winchester's house.

An aura of mystery and dark foreboding surrounds the awesome structure. The towering spires, minarets and cupolas stand dark and still silhouetted against the sky. Inside there are trap doors, secret passageways and doors which open into the air.

The Gothic Victorian is a living monument to the dead. The legend of Sarah Winchester, who tried to shut out the grim realities of life and death with a carpenter's hammer, is everywhere.

The story of Sarah Winchester—surely the most enigmatic woman in the history of the West—is a fascinating one, as is the legend of the house itself. To the pioneers of the 19th century, the Winchester repeating rifle was "the gun that won the West." But to Sarah Pardee Winchester, heiress to the fortune of the Winchester Repeating Arms Co., the weapon was an instrument of doom and ultimate destruction for herself.

According to the story, the widow of the rifle manufacturer's only son was informed by a Boston medium that the spirits of those killed by Winchester rifles had placed a curse upon her. The medium advised Sarah that she might escape the curse by moving west and building a house. As long as the building continued, the vengeful spirits would be thwarted and Sarah would live.

The unhappy heiress obediently moved to California and purchased an eight-room farmhouse which she proceeded to remodel literally as the spirit moved her. The construction project, begun in 1884, was to occupy the next thirty-eight years of her life and would ultimately employ hundreds of artisans working on a 'round the clock basis that included Sundays and holidays.

An early addition was a tower, housing a huge bell, but with no way of getting to it except by climbing over roofs and placing ladders against the side.   Inside the tower was a smooth, unscalable well, down the center of which hung the bell rope.   It was through an underground passage, known only to one servant and his understudy, that the end of the rope could be reached.

The bell ringer always carried an expensive watch. Every day he telephoned an observatory and checked the correctness of his chronometers, from which, in turn, he set his watch. The bell rang only at midnight and 2 a. m. — an occurrence that puzzled neighbors for years. Later it was learned that these were the hours when Sarah's spectral guests arrived and departed.

Aerial view of the Winchester Mystery House.
Photograph reprinted courtesy of Winchester Mystery House

Design conferences took place in the seance room where the lady of the house retired each night. Just before midnight Sarah donned a gown etched with occult designs to prepare for her nightly seance. After slipping through her Victorian labyrinth, she pressed a button, and a panel slid open enabling her to step quickly from one apartment to the next. Following yet another maze, she came to the Blue Room with its thirteen coat hooks and emerged just as the bell tolled twelve.

For the next two hours she would await ghostly instructions.   Her spectral consultants were capricious and insatiable, demanding room after room, balcony after balcony, chimney after chimney. The strange growth spread until it reached a distant barn, flowed around and adhered to it like a tumor, and finally engulfed it.   An observation tower

SOUTH BAY & CENTRAL CALIFORNIA

shot up, only to be choked by later construction until nothing could be seen from it.

To the original eight rooms, hundreds were added, many of them quickly ripped out to make way for new ideas from Mrs. Winchester's nocturnal advisors. Today, one hundred and sixty rooms of this baffling labyrinth still stand, the survivors of an estimated seven hundred and fifty chambers interconnected—if one can use that term—by trick doors, self intersecting balconies and dead-end stairways.

Literally miles of winding, twisting, bewildering corridors snake through the house while numerous secret passageways are concealed in the walls. Some end in closets, others in blank walls. The door from one was the rear wall of a walk-in icebox. The halls vary in width from two feet to regulation size and some ceilings are so low that an average size person must stoop to avoid bumping his head.

The explanation for all this is that the house was devised by ghosts for ghosts. If ghost stories are to be believed, spirits dearly love to vanish up chimneys. So Sarah obligingly provided them with not one but forty-seven of these escape hatches.

Sarah Winchester

The lonely widow was obviously intrigued by the number thirteen as well as by other aspects of the occult. Nearly every column in the house—from the mahogany newell post inlaid with rosewood in the hallway to the uprights supporting the porch roof—was carefully inverted and installed upside down. The interior courtyard contained a hedge cut into the ancient half moon symbol. Sarah's greenhouse had thirteen cupolas, there were thirteen palms lining the driveway, thirteen lights on the chandeliers, ceilings with thirteen panels, rooms with thirteen windows, thirteen bathrooms, and thirteen drainage holes in the kitchen sink. Whenever possible the number thirteen seems to have been incorporated or its multiples (26, 39, 52). There are even thirteen parts to Sarah's will —yes, her signature appears thirteen times!

Dining in splendor with her secretary-companion, Mrs. Winchester frequently enjoyed the best vintage wines. One evening she went to the wine cellar—to which only she possessed the key—to locate a special bottle. To her horror, she discovered a black handprint on the wall. That night the spirits confided that it was the print of a demon's hand. Sarah took this as a warning against alcohol and had the cellar walled up so thoroughly that, to this day, the liquid treasures have never been found.

The seance room where Sarah received her instructions was off limits to other humans. Those entering the forbidden sanctuary after her death found only a small blue room furnished with a cabinet, armchair, table, paper and planchette board for automatic writing.

The capricious mistress of the manor indulged her whimsey by never sleeping in the same bedroom for two consecutive nights. In this way

The ballroom at the Winchester Mystery House. Photograph by Joe Melena.

she hoped to confuse unwanted spirits, but it was her servants who were confused after the 1906 earthquake. Following the severe tremor it took the staff nearly an hour to finally locate their frightened mistress who had been trapped inside a room when the wall shifted, jamming the door.

Sarah believed the terrifying experience had been inflicted upon her as a punishment for her extravagance in constructing the front of the house. To placate the spirits, she ordered the front thirty rooms sealed off and never used. This included the grand ballroom which had been built at a cost of $9000 and a stained glass window costing $2000. The exorbitantly priced front door was used by only three people — Sarah Winchester and the two carpenters who installed it.

Yet money was hardly a concern. In addition to an initial inheritance of $20 million, Sarah had received 48.8 percent of Winchester Repeating Arms Company stock, giving her an income of $1000 a day (tax-free until 1913).

Despite all her efforts, death came to Sarah Winchester on September 5, 1922. Today one can still see half-driven nails where the carpenters stopped when word came that the eighty-five year old recluse had died quietly in her sleep.

The widow spent more than $5.5 million to please her discarnate friends. Unless ghosts are unspeakable ingrates, Mrs. Winchester should have been well received on the other side.

But was that the end of the story? Hardly, to judge from the weird tales surrounding the house. Over the years a variety of psychic phenomena have been reported—chains rattling, door knobs turning by themselves, windows and doors opening and closing by themselves, whispers, footsteps—a Gothic thriller seemingly come to life.

In order to investigate these claims, the Nirvana Foundation obtained permission to spend a night in the house. There were five in our party: Dal and Sylvia Brown; Dick Schaskey, head of the photography department at San Jose State University; Ann Fockelmann, a research associate at the foundation; and me.

Sylvia Brown at the Winchester Mystery House..
Photograph by A. May.

Throughout the long night Sylvia, Ann and I saw moving lights for which we could not account. All of us felt sudden gusts of icy wind and cold spots. While sitting in the bedroom where Mrs.

Sarah Winchester — photograph taken secretly by a gardener.
Reprinted courtesy of the Winchester Mystery House.

Winchester died, Sylvia and I saw great balls of red light that seemed to explode before us.

As the rest of us sat on the floor of the bedroom clutching our clipboards and cameras, Sylvia saw a couple whom, she claimed, watched us intently from across the room.

During the thirty-eight years that Sarah Winchester resided in the "mystery house," her servants and other employees remained fiercely loyal, defending her every eccentricity. They described her as strong-minded and firm, but always fair and kind. Each was well paid and some were rewarded with lifetime pensions or real estate.

In death, it would appear that Mrs. Winchester received the same attention from her servants as when she was alive. "The man and woman that I see are dressed in clothing popular during the turn of the century," Sylvia explained. "They're caretakers, I think. Their attitude isn't really menacing but they are watching us very carefully. They don't seem to like strangers in their house."

As the night wore on the frightening sense of being observed did not diminish. We sat for about an hour watching a ghostly shadow play across the dark walls. Each of us tried to explain the spectral light show in earthly terms. Moonlight? There was no moon. Passing cars? The few windows faced onto a dark courtyard. There were no cars.

It was a very long night.

A daylight bustle had settled over the place as we wearily carried out our equipment the next morning. Maintenance of so large a structure never stops. The sounds one hears during the day are anything but spectral. The carpenter's hammer echoes just as it did during the mansion's heyday.

So it would seem that Sarah Winchester does, indeed, live on as her home does—achieving its own kind of immortality.

The Winchester House, located at 525 South Winchester Blvd. just off I-280 in San Jose, is open to visitors every day but Christmas. Daily guided tours are offered and special events planned on Halloween and on every Friday the 13th. Telephone: (408) 247-2000.

THE GHOST IN THE HAUNTED TOY STORE

Toys R Us hasn't yet put up a sign warning, "Beware of Flying Teddy Bears," but it may well come to that.

Marcie Honey with "talking" doll at Toys R Us.   Photograph by C.J. Marrow.

A toy tipped off the staff that something was wrong, but this was only the beginning of a weird set of circumstances verified by a leading California psychic.

The ghostly games began with a talking doll that couldn't. A customer returned the toy to cashier Margie Honey, complaining that it was defective. Honey tilted the doll this way and that, but no sound would come. Satisfied that nothing could be done, she placed the toy in a carton, intending to return it to the manufacturer. No sooner had she closed the lid than the doll began to cry, "Mama!"

"After this happened a few times it ceased to be funny," Honey recalls. "I began to feel that the doll had a will of its own. Finally I called a clerk and asked him to take the toy away. It cried all the way to the stockroom."

A few nights later, Honey was sitting alone in the employee lounge. Suddenly a large bulletin board secured to the wall began to swing back and forth. Then a stack of papers on top of the refrigerator fluttered to the floor—one by one. There was no fan or ventilator system that could account for this, she says.

SOUTH BAY & CENTRAL CALIFORNIA

Charlie Brown, another Toys R Us employee, had a brush with the supernatural one evening while closing up. He had just locked the door when he heard a banging sound from the inside. Brown returned to the building, unlocked the door and entered—there was no one inside. He closed and locked the door and the banging started once more. The pattern continued several times until he finally gave up and walked away, the frantic pounding echoing in his ears.

Regina Gibson, a clerk, tells of hearing her name called again and again while she was alone in the customer service area and of feeling something running its fingers through her long hair while she was perched on a high ladder stocking shelves.

Judy Jackson, a former store manager, was confronted by a customer who complained, "There's something strange going on in the women's restroom."

Jackson listened in amazement as the customer explained, "I turned off the water faucet, but by the time I reached the door it had turned itself on again. I went back and turned it off, only to have it turn on again. This happened three times and now it's on again."

One evening just before closing time, Bill Peevan, another employee carefully stacked a group of shoe skates on a shelf. He was the last one out of the building. The next morning he returned to find them rearranged in an intricate pattern—on the floor.

This and other similar cases of merchandise or equipment being moved during the night is particularly curious. The store—more of a warehouse than a traditional toy shop—is well organized. Everything is kept in an assigned place and the nightly closing follows a regimented pattern.

Once the customers leave, the entire floor is dry mopped. A security man checks to see that everything is accounted for and in place. Then all the employees leave at once with the security agent who locks the door. If any attempt is made to open the door before 9:30 a.m. an elaborate alarm system is triggered automatically notifying the police.

Many of the employees have come to believe that well-secured shelves unaccountably falling, footsteps heard in empty lofts, and lights turning themselves on and off can mean only one thing—a ghost. But of whom—or what?

When Margie Honey and Regina Gibson decided to investigate, their search took them to the Sunnyvale Library. Among the archives was a cryptic note which read, "It is said that the ghost of Martin Murphy is seen on nights of the full moon."

The note has since mysteriously disappeared from the library, but the legend of Martin Murphy persists.

Descended from the kings of Ireland, Murphy, the founding father of the cities of Sunnyvale, Mountain View and Los Altos, carved his own empire in the Santa Clara Valley. One of the very first settlers to reach California, his were the first wheel tracks from the mid section of the western states across the Sierra Mountains. His trail, forged in 1844, would later be the route used by the first transcontinental railroad.

Settling in what would eventually be Sunnyvale, Murphy purchased the 5000-acre Pastoria de las Borregas, a Spanish land grant rancho that stretched from what is now Lawrence Expressway to Mountain View.

Martin Murphy

Within ten years, Murphy's holdings had doubled and his home was the valley's showplace. Described as a "white ship in a golden sea of grain," the Murphy mansion had been shipped in pieces around the Horn and then assembled like sections of a jigsaw puzzle.

On July 18, 1881, Martin and Mary Murphy celebrated their Golden Wedding Anniversary. Concerned lest he slight someone, Murphy published an open invitation to the entire county in the *San Jose Mercury*. The Board of Supervisors adjourned to attend the affair, as did the judge, jury, witnesses and counsel of a Superior Court trial. They joined an estimated 10,000 guests who partied for three days and nights. Not surprisingly, the gala was described by a San Francisco paper as "the most fabulous social event ever held in California."

Some say the Murphy saga didn't end with Murphy's death in 1884. Many past and present employees of Toys R Us believe that his is a restless spirit still bound to earthly pleasures. They call their resident ghost "Martin" and consider him friendly, if mischievous.

However, this could also be a description of the corporeal Murphy — a man well known for his conviviality and Irish sense of humor. Having been actively involved with the city from the beginning, it's easy to imagine a continuing interest in the present day community.

Murphy was a doting family man who named the city streets for his numerous offspring: Taafee Avenue and Yuba Street for his daughter, Elizabeth Yuba Murphy Taafee (born on the banks of the Yuba River, the first child born to American settlers in California), Mary Avenue and Carroll Street for Mary Ann Murphy Carroll, Helen and Argue Avenues for Helen Murphy Argue, Mathilda, Maude and Beverly Avenues for granddaughters.

But interest in young people extended beyond his own family. Murphy helped found Santa Clara University and the College of Notre Dame at Belmont.

In hopes of meeting "Martin," a group of psychic researchers, including this writer, spent one very long night at Toys R Us. Entering as the last shoppers were ushered out, we observed the regimented closing procedure from the inside. Merchandise was checked and straightened, floors mopped, employees checked out, and the doors locked. We would not be able to leave without triggering the alarm system.

During the night, a giant bop bag set well back on a shelf tumbled to the floor—seemingly of its own volition. Several balls belonging on the

Flying bop bag. Toys R Us. Photograph by C.J. Marrow

shelves on aisle 107 appeared on the floor of aisle 206. Later that night a weighted ball was found in the center of a corridor and was put back on its shelf and barricaded in place by a box. Within an hour the ball was back on the floor again—the box pushed to one side.

The star of the research team was Sylvia Brown, co- founder of the Campbell-based Nirvana Foundation, who attempted to psychically "tune in" to the store. To everyone's surprise, she began to describe not Martin Murphy, but a circuit

Sylvia Brown at Toys R Us.　　Photograph by C.J. Marrow.

preacher whom she "saw" brooding over an unrequited love.

The preacher's name, she said, was John or Yon Johnson. She saw him clearly pumping water from a spring which appeared to her as bubbling out of a corner of the store. Yon stayed with a family who resided on the property, she explained. He fell in love with one of the daughters, a pretty girl named Elizabeth, but she was scarcely aware of his existence. Elizabeth married someone else; Yon or John remained a bachelor. Brown also spoke of tremendous activity within the area in the years 1881 and 1923.

It was a long night and at times a scary one as we sat in the darkness listening as Sylvia Brown described the lovelorn preacher whom she believes continues to roam the store which he still sees as a farm and orchard.

The next day the team began the difficult task of trying to validate Brown's psychic findings. Could Sylvia Brown's Elizabeth be Martin Murphy's daughter, Elizabeth Yuba Murphy Taaffee?

1881 was the year of the wedding anniversary party but what of 1923? Newspaper accounts of the time failed to turn up anything of note; but then, for what were we searching?

There was a preacher, we discovered, one John Johnson—known as "Yonny"—who boarded with his parishioners and undoubtedly spent time on the property now occupied by the toy store. Yonny did, indeed, die a bachelor. A spring, now capped, flowed where the building stands. Quite likely, Yonny pumped water there.

Craig Schriner, Channel 2 photographer, shooting Sylvia Brown while in trance.   Photograph by Bill Tidwell.

Possibly the most startling thing to come out of the toy shop seance was the weird light show of dancing blobs captured on film by Oakland photographer Bill Tidwell. Was the phenomenon caused by lens flare or was this one more supernatural joke?

"Should we call him Martin or Yonny?" Mary Ringo, the new store manager, is frequently asked by her staff. Whoever he may be, Mary is quite certain that the ghost exists. Frequently during busy seasons it's necessary for Ringo to stay late in the evening supervising a crew of some nine to twelve staff members. "All of us have heard footsteps walking in the unoccupied floor above us — it's practically a nightly occurrence.

And the water faucets—well, that's really a problem in drought years. They turn on so often that we have to keep checking all the time."

Whatever his identity, Mary and her employees have grown quite fond of their spirit connection. One thing's certain, they've no intention of giving up the ghost.

Toys R Us is located in Sunnyvale on the corner of El Camino Real and Saratoga-Sunnyvale Road. Telephone: (408) 732-0331

SOUTH BAY & CENTRAL CALIFORNIA

PACHECO PASS

Residents and officials of Santa Clara and San Benito counties routinely urge the rerouting of treacherous Highway 152, the road that has claimed the lives of nearly 200 people in the past decade alone.

The heavily traveled highway through the Coast Range between Los Banos and Gilroy has a history of tragedy that reaches back nearly two centuries. In the early 1800s, the Indians called the Pacheco pass the "Trail of Tears," for it was their avenue of escape from the harsh rule of Father Felipe Arroyo who held them enslaved at Mission San Juan Bautista. Many of his "neophytes," unlucky enough to be caught were beaten and dragged back in chains to the mission by the Spanish padres who depended upon them for a cheap labor force to maintain their feudal empire. Casa de Fruta, now a popular tourist attraction, marks the site of an artesian well where the Indians once stopped to refresh themselves before beginning the hazardous trek.

The pass gets its name from the Francisco Pacheco family who received it in 1843 as part of a 150,000 acre land grant. It was thought by the Mexican government that the presence of Don Francisco, a gun carriage maker, might be a deterrent to Indians — freed at last from bondage by the secularization of the missions — who resented the settlers now pouring into their land.

But Indians weren't the only menace to new arrivals. With the Gold Rush came the bandits, Joaquin Murieta and Tiburcio Vasquez among the most notorious. In 1851 Pacheco moved his family from "the wilds" to Monterey. The violence remained. And, if anything, the coming of "civilization" only intensified it. Cars began to navigate the winding pass in the 1920s and soon the unprecedented accident rate caused the area to be known as "blood alley."

On January 30, 1977 Sylvia and Dal Brown were returning from a short vacation at Palm Springs. It was 6:30 p. m. and they had just reached Pacheco Pass on Highway 152.

They were passing San Luis Dam when unaccountably their good humored banter ceased. Sylvia felt suddenly overcome with anxiety. As a lifelong medium, she has had countless brushes with the supernatural, but nothing comparable to this wave of sheer panic.

Sylvia glanced at her husband. He seemed oblivious to the turmoil that had enveloped her so completely. "This is what hell must be," she thought and started to pray. But prayer only increased Sylvia's discomfort; she could recall nothing beyond, "Our Father." It seemed now that hundreds of voices were assailing her consciousness, strident, angry voices without words. Sylvia felt that she had been plunged into an endless void of pain and terror which seemed to have no beginning and no end.

"Help me!" she gasped, clutching Dal's arm.

"What is it, honey, tell me?" Later she learned that he had repeated the words again and again, finally shouting them when she failed to respond. Sylvia had never heard him answer.

Dal, unable to pull off the road, continued to drive. Her sense of terror increased as images began to appear. She saw a little girl in a covered wagon cowering with her fists pressed against her eyes while Indians raged around the wagon train. Her sense of hopelessness was overwhelming. Scenes from a series of battles followed involving Spaniards, Mexicans, American settlers—all passing before her eyes in brutal succession.

"Those visions seemed to possess me, reason was useless," she said later. "Finally, as we reached the restaurant, Casa de Fruta, they began to subside, but an intense depression replaced them.

"In an effort to reach out, I talked endlessly of the experience to my family and associates at the Nirvana Foundation. They were inclined to

SOUTH BAY & CENTRAL CALIFORNIA

write it off as a psychic impression — well, I've had *those* all my life. It was more than that, it had to be. Somewhere along the lonely stretch of highway known as Pacheco Pass lurks something very real, very negative and very dangerous."

The intensity of Sylvia's impressions led her to believe that others must have shared the same experiences. The flood of stories that followed her lectures confirmed this suspicion. The following are quotations taken from affidavits filed with the Nirvana foundation:

> *"In many years of going over the Pacheco Pass there has always been a deep feeling of desperate anticipation that something was going to happen to me. Also, I would have the most awful thoughts of death."*

* * *

> *"I felt totally lost and I didn't care about anything, but there was a very strong sense of fear. I knew I shouldn't be scared. . .but I can't even explain how I felt other than to say lost, panicked, and very dizzy."*

* * *

> *"While traveling Pacheco Pass as a passenger on a very rainy night I became extremely frightened about going around the curves, although the driver was driving normally, I became really excited and asked the driver to stop for no apparent reason. We stopped and I became even more excited; we finally drove on and the feeling subsided."*

* * *

> *"Saw lights in the sky and had a horrible feeling of being trapped. My husband was asleep and I felt totally alone and alienated. I felt I couldn't get away."*

* * *

"The drive up Interstate 5 was boring and uneventful. However the ride from I-5 to highway 101, on Pacheco Pass was a nightmare I never want to relive. I have been driving for 30 years, day and night, in all kinds of weather. I have never had any fear of darkness or of driving alone. But that night on Pacheco Pass, I drove in a state of sheer panic.

"I became paranoid, feeling as if all the other cars were 'out to get me'—the ones approaching and the ones coming up behind me. I wanted to pull off the road, but couldn't. I wanted to drive slower, but seemed to be pushed and pulled by the other cars and trucks to go faster and faster. I can never remember feeling such terror for such a long period of time. I truly felt that my death was imminent."

* * *

To these, I must add my own experience. Driving the Pacheco Pass one warm September evening, I experienced total, unexplained, unaccountable panic. Stranger yet, I couldn't get the idea out of my mind that I was being menaced by Indians. My fears began to dissipate after passing Casa de Fruta, but the depression remained for several days.

The most striking aspect of the phenomenon is this high degree of emotional involvement. All accounts refer to the anxiety experienced with no apparent cause. Sylvia Brown talks of a "nameless terror." Her intellectual control was blocked; not even simple prayers could be recalled. Terms that reappear in numerous accounts are "void," "alienated," "death," and "trapped."

Subsequent discussions with Sylvia uncovered another factor. A distortion of the local time structure seems to occur. She reports losing an hour while driving through the area. Two other persons experienced a time distortion. Their account reads:

SOUTH BAY & CENTRAL CALIFORNIA

"When we got to Fresno (from San Jose) and checked the time, we found that we had made the trip forty-five minutes faster than we ever had before. On the way back we lost an hour."

* * *

An interesting point to note is that the experience occurred on January 30, 1977—the same day of Sylvia's encounter.

Sylvia believes the phenomenon is caused by an energy implant. This, she surmises, is a collection of highly charged emotional experiences that have occurred in the area. Over the years the energy from intense emotions has collected and become self-sustaining. This energy, if sufficiently strong, causes a warp in the psycho-emotional structure of space-time. The warp acts like a gravitational field, pulling other waves of emotion.

The whirling boundary can be crossed; but, once inside, the rational mind may be totally overwhelmed by negative energy. Nothing is connected to time: it is all happening now—an eternal play. The foundation of one's reality slips away leaving only a sense of utter futility.

What could have caused such an implant?

Can it be the violent history of the area—the numerous battles involving Indians, Spaniards, Mexicans, American settlers, highwaymen, and the many public hangings? Violence continues to this day in the form of numerous automobile accidents.

What obsession leads a driver to speed on a mountain highway? Could it be a compulsion to get out of there as quickly as possible? California Highway Patrol officers interviewed blamed "emotions" for many of the accidents and referred to survivors as "paranoid." A surprising number become involved in violent quarrels. An attempt to cut off or block another car may trigger a kind of war. Bumper tag may erupt into violent fist fights — or a fatal accident.

The CHP says this irrational behavior occurs frequently on the pass. One patrolman remarked. "They're all trying to die quick up there. They're all crazy."

Suicide seems to be another not infrequent cause of death on the pass. People appear to run off the edge of the road for no apparent reason. A CHP lieutenant said, "I know people who won't drive through Pacheco Pass because they're scared to death of it."

With very good reason, it would seem.

Pacheco Pass is located on Highway 152 between I-5 and Highway 101.

SOUTH BAY & CENTRAL CALIFORNIA

How much does a man
    live, after all?
Does he live a thousand
    days, or one only?
For a week, or for several
    centuries?
How long does a man
    spend dying?

                — Pablo Neruda

THE MOTHER LODE COUNTRY

THE VINEYARD HOUSE

THE SUTTER CREEK INN

NEVADA COUNTY HISTORICAL MUSEUM

THE WILLOW HOTEL

THE LANEY HOUSE

THE VINEYARD HOUSE

Louise Allhoff must have been a hard woman to live with.

There was a first husband, a successful vintner, who committed suicide in a Virginia City outhouse.

Then along came Robert Chalmers, the merchant prince of the Gold Rush capital, Coloma. Attracted to the beautiful widow with her easy elegance and proud, imperious ways, Chalmers persuaded her to marry him. For a time they were a formidable team. Chalmers had the hustle, Louise had the class. They enlarged her vineyards and won prizes for their wines. Chalmers was elected to the State legislature. While his financial empire continued to grow, she introduced "culture" to the area.

At the apex of their success, this pair of high rollers constructed a four-story mansion which was to be a mecca for the Mother Lode elite. Among the attractions of their "Vineyard House" was a ninety-foot ballroom and a music room.

But Robert Chalmers' pleasure was brief. Soon after completion of the showplace in 1878, his manner began to change. The former orator now spoke in whispers. Seeing a grave being dug in the cemetery across the street, he walked over and laid down to see if it would fit him.

The Vineyard House. Photograph by C. J. Marrow.

Soon—according to Louise — Chalmers was a raving maniac and she was forced to chain him in the cellar of their home. It was said that she came down often to taunt him, standing always just beyond his frenzied grasp. Chalmers' misery lasted for nearly three years. In 1881, he starved to death, fearing that Louise was trying to poison him.

Call it divine retribution or merely bad luck, hard times befell Louise. A blight attacked her grapes. The Chinese immigrants who slept in the vineyard to keep deer out were expelled in a pogrom and the remaining grapes ravaged by humans and animals. Their real estate holdings had dwindled during Chalmers' illness and the bank foreclosed on the Vineyard House.

Louise was allowed to remain on a rent paying basis; but, in order to do so, was forced to take in roomers and to allow the cellar to be used as an auxiliary jail. At least two prisoners spent their last night on earth there. One was a school teacher who had killed a student, the other a highwayman. The teacher recited poetry from the scaffold, the highwayman danced a jig and then burst into tears.

Louise died, lonely and impoverished, in 1913. The proud mansion where Ulysses S. Grant once made a speech fell into melancholy decay as a series of owners came and went, always complaining of unaccountable sounds. One tenant left suddenly in the middle of the night, refusing to talk about what he'd seen.

The bar in the cellar jail.
Photograph by C.J. Marrow

In 1956 the house was turned into an inn and restaurant. Drinks are now served in the cellar jail where thieves, murderers and Robert Chalmers once languished. Dave Vanbuskirk, one of the owners, often heard unexplained steps on the stairs and seen a doorknob turn before his startled eyes — with no one on the other side. Once in the seemingly empty house a freshly made bed came unmade and the impression of a form could clearly be seen on the sheets. The fact that Vanbuskirk had, himself,

THE MOTHER LODE COUNTRY

found a stack of old coffins under the front porch shortly after buying the place did little to cheer him.

Louise & Robert Chalmers are buried in this pioneer graveyard across the street from the Vineyard House.

Photograph by A. May.

During the night guests reported hearing the sound of chains rattling, rustling skirts, heavy breathing and brisk steps. One San Francisco couple heard a raucous group enter by the front door and climb the stairs laughing loudly. Going to the door to quiet the revelers, they saw three men dressed in Victorian clothing fade before their eyes.

Darlene and Frank Herrera, who purchased the house in 1974, tried to play down the "ghost stuff." They worked hard to make the place genuinely Victorian with a variety of museum quality antiques.

Yet what could they say in 1987 when a Sacramento couple packed their bags in the middle of the night, drove to Placerville and reported to the sheriff that someone was being murdered in the next room? Investigators subsequently found nothing.

Frank, a retired sheet metal worker and avowed skeptic, was bar tending one night when two wine glasses slid across the bar on their own—as though moved by unseen hands.

That night the staff gathered after closing as Frank and Darlene sat down with a Ouija across their knees. After nearly a half hour of concentration, the Ouija pointer began to move indicating a spirit presence. "Who are you?" Darlene asked.

Moving from letter to letter the pointer spelled out the name G-E-O-R-G-E. The assembled group asked a variety of questions. Answers were chatty and a tad mischievous—not too surprising when the spirit at last explained that he was only two years old.

But that's not the end of the story. Two days later Kay Morton, a Placerville artist, had dinner at the Vineyard House with a group of friends. It was her first visit.

At dinner, Morton says, she felt the presence of a small boy who asked her to mash his carrots and give him a cracker. Her companions saw nothing, but later in the evening Morton asked the bartender, Patty Backhaus, if there was a very small boy named George living in the house. Backhaus, who'd watched the Ouija activity, nearly dropped the drink she was serving.

Kay Morton, unable to get the experience out of her mind, returned to the Vineyard House a few days later. She wanted to walk through the building when it was quiet. Upon entering Room No. 5 on the second floor, Morton was "overcome by a sense of fear and pain." "It was," she said, "as if spirits were trying to get out of the room."

Frank and Darlene could only look at one another in shocked disbelief. Room No. 5 was the same room where the Sacramento couple had heard sounds of the phantom murder.

In June 1991, Cindy and Paul Savage bought the Vineyard House and are busy with ongoing renovations. A volunteer assistant is Dave Wieser, who admits to a love affair with Louise that transcends time and space.

Despite Louise's rather sinister reputation, Wieser is pleased about the birthday both share—November 11—and throws a party on that date each year. He also carries a coin in his pocket dating back to the last century. Just in case he's transported back in time, he'll be able to take Louise for a buggy ride.

The Vineyard House is located off Highway 49 and Coldsprings Road in Coloma. Telephone: (916) 622-2217

THE MOTHER LODE COUNTRY

THE SUTTER CREEK INN

The Sutter Creek Inn is alive with ghosts—both nice and naughty.

Not only does the house—a New England clapboard—attract phenomena, so does its owner, Jane Way.

Jane bought the house in 1966. "Just why, I can't imagine," she says today. "It was an all time low in my life. My son had been killed in an accident. My husband and I had just split. My health was terrible—I'd had cancer twice. I was feeling very, very sorry for myself."

Soon after, while passing through San Francisco, she stopped on an impulse at a spiritualist church. "It was a crazy thing to do," she admits. "I was just driving down a street looking for an on-ramp to the freeway and saw the sign. I'd never been there before, never had known anyone who had—but suddenly there I was parking my car and walking in."

"The minister was Florence Becker, a very gifted medium. We'd never met before. Of course she couldn't have known a thing about me—and yet she seemed to know everything. 'You've just lost your son,' she said almost immediately and then began to describe him in detail. Her description was so accurate that I began to cry.'

"'You've bought an old place in the mountains,' she continued. 'I see people coming and going—it must be a hotel. That's right for you—but you must stop the bitterness. It could ruin everything. Keep on with what you're doing but without bitterness. You'll be successful.'"

Jane Way left the church and drove back to Sutter Creek. Again and again her mind returned to the medium's words. Then a few nights later she saw her first ghost.

"It was Saturday evening and all the hotel guests were out," she recalls.

"I was getting ready to leave also; some friends were having a costume party. Suddenly conscious of being watched, I looked up. There was a tall man wearing old fashioned looking clothes standing in the doorway. For a moment I thought he must be going to the same party. I heard the words: *I will protect your inn.* He smiled and then faded away.

"Well, really, how could I be bitter after an experience like that? Surely somebody out of this world had decided to take an interest in my affairs. What more could anyone ask? I suppose what had bothered me most was the apparent futility of life, its seeming transience. Now here in my own house was living proof of the continuity of the human spirit."

Way believes that this was the spirit of State Senator Edward Convers Voorhies who had lived in the house for many years.

The Sutter Creek Inn. Photograph by C.J. Marrow.

The house had originally been built in 1860 by John Keyes as a home for his young bride, Clara McIntire. It was hoped its New England lines would ease the loneliness for her native New Hampshire. The couple had one child who died of diphtheria when still a baby. Then in 1875

Keyes died leaving Clara a widow at thirty-four.

Two years later Voorhies came to town and proceeded to court her. They were married on March 29, 1880. The couple had two children. Earl died in infancy, but Gertrude lived to be ninety.

"I bought the house from Gertrude just before she moved to a rest home," Way explains. "She'd lived in the place all her life and was very attached to it. I suppose that's why her spirit returned one evening as several guests were gathered in the living room—she just wanted to check on things."

Way's experience with Senator Voorhies, following so soon after the psychic reading, seems to have triggered a mediumship within herself. In the intervening years she experienced a wide variety of psychic phenomena.

There was a German ophthalmologist who tried to help me with an eye problem. He didn't—but I know his intentions were good," she says.

Way's less certain about a spectral exhibitionist—a flasher. "He seemed very proud of his endowments," she recalls. "I think he'd been punished in some way in his earthly life, possibly been mutilated. You'd think death would be the end of earthly hang-ups; but, if he's any indication, we take them with us.

"Once a cat was flung against the wall by an unseen force—possibly a ghost who doesn't like cats. They don't like garlic either, I've discovered. If you don't want ghosts, a good fettuccine should eliminate any chance of an encounter."

A very good remedy to keep in mind.

The Sutter Creek Inn is located at 75 Main Street, Sutter Creek. Telephone: (209) 267-5606.

NEVADA COUNTY HISTORICAL MUSEUM

"The equipment of the Nevada County Fire Department is not to be excelled by that of any similar organization in any town of the same size on the Pacific Slope. The town is well supplied with hydrants and the water pressure is strong enough to throw a stream over the highest buildings."

The Nevada City Transcript had good reason to boast that March morning in 1877. A well equipped fire department meant life itself to the tinderbox towns of the Mother Lode.

Firehouse No. 1 had been built in 1861. The Victorian bell tower and gingerbread trim were added a few years later. The facility continued in use until 1938. Ten years later it was converted into a museum by the Nevada County Historical Society.

Nevada County Historical Museum.
Photograph by C.J. Marrow.

But the excitement was by no means over. As antiques and artifacts arrived—so did something else. Something with an ornery desire to push people around.

Hjalmer E. Berg, director of the museum, reports inexplicable footsteps and cold air currents. "Many times I've been in the museum but known that I wasn't alone," he says.

Once Rebecca Miller, president of the historical society, tried to shut a cabinet door. "As fast as I could close the door, it would fly back open,"

THE MOTHER LODE COUNTRY

Hjalner E. Berg..   Photo by C.J. Marrow

she recalls. "Finally I said aloud, 'Stop this, I don't have time!' "It stopped, but then I heard footsteps behind me. I turned, but there was no one there." (Surely a classic case of a ghost having the last word.)

Berg tells of a time when a Jesuit priest and two graduate students were touring the otherwise empty museum. They ascended the stairs to the second floor and returned almost immediately. "Are you playing a joke on us?" the priest asked. It seemed that a redhaired "floozy" in old fashioned finery had startled them by appearing out of nowhere, sitting down at the piano—a relic from an old whorehouse—and began to plink away.

"It didn't help at all to tell him that we had no such woman employed at the museum — which, of course, we don't. The idea of a spectral volunteer was even more alarming than a prostitute."

Another time a group of Business and Professional Women were visiting the museum. They'd examined everything on the first level and had just climbed the stairs to the second floor when all of a sudden one woman began to scream. "They're after me!" she shrieked, running down the stairs and out the front door. No one was ever able to learn what had frightened her so."

One of the most interesting features within the museum is an 1880 photograph of an Irish miner named Carrigan. The subject is a mature, white-bearded man, but to the side of the photograph is the image of a boy of about twelve.

Photograph by C.J. Marrow.

According to the story, Carrigan told the astonished photographer that as the picture was taken he was thinking rather nostalgically of his boyhood. It would seem that these thoughts somehow transmitted themselves to the film, emerging as his own youthful countenance. As the years pass the boy seems to be growing clearer. Some see other faces in the photograph as well.

Medium Nick Nocerino says these other faces are Chinese ghosts. Nocerino came to the museum at Berg's request to exorcise the place when the phenomena seemed to be taking on a more hostile character.

Both men believed that the evil influence was emanating from the thousand year old Taoist shrine at one end of the museum. The shrine had been taken from a Grass Valley joss house—joss meaning god—and is believed to be the oldest of its kind in North America.

Photograph by C.J. Marrow.

As visitors to the museum stood in front of the shrine, many experienced the sensation of being pushed or shoved. A few said they felt as if someone was trying to trip them.

Attendance at the museum was dwindling and Berg—proud of the historic displays he'd worked so hard to accumulate—was concerned.

Nocerino was able to tune in psychically to the situation, making contact with two Chinese spirits who admitted that they had been tripping pagans who got too close to their sacred altar.

Nocerino performed an exorcism ceremony to dispatch the ghosts. Berg put up a rail to discourage the guests. Between the two of them, things are back to "normal" at the museum.

The Nevada County Historical Museum is located on Main Street in Nevada City. Telephone: (916) 265-5468

THE WILLOW HOTEL

First it was the site of a lynching—a man was summarily hung. Later there were at least three violent deaths triggered by the pressures of frontier life. Finally there was a mine disaster killing twenty-three men.

Small wonder that the Willow Hotel built in 1862 on the site of these tragedies—collapsed mine shaft, lynching and violence resulting in multiple deaths—would have questionable vibes.

The Willow Hotel circa 1862.

But there's even another reason. Psychic researcher and medium, Nick Nocerino says that the most likely cause of the chronic fires that have plagued the building — at least five of them in the last decade — was the Jamestown Fire of 1896. In that dreadful holocaust, the town had no water to fight the fire, so locals resorted to dynamite to stifle the flames. Most of the town was devastated—save the Willow Hotel.

Nocerino believes that that long ago bad luck has triggered an enduring resentment among the ghosts of people who were killed in the blaze and subsequent explosions.

In an attempt to placate them, the medium conducted an exorcism of the building. Nine spirits were contacted on October 1978. "I could reason with six of them," he told me, "but there are three others who are still angry. I'm afraid they'll be back and they'll take something else with them."

Sadly enough Nocerino's prediction came true. On July 20, 1985 yet another mystery blaze not only destroyed the hotel annex, but a nearby barbershop, jewelry store and food market. The fire began with what appeared to have been an overheated refrigerator and then went straight up to the Hanging Room on the second floor, the first room to burn. The "hanging room," — dark, spooky hardly more than a closet — got its name from the deaths of two men, strangers to one another, who hung themselves there on two consecutive nights.

Many priceless antiques were consumed by flames. The building, thought to be the oldest surviving hotel in the Mother Lode constructed totally of wood, was gutted. Amazingly, the ancient bar constructed of exquisitely joined mahogany, rosewood and redwood burl, where the infamous gun slinger Bat Masterson had once lounged, remained intact.

During the efforts to re-construct the building, Mike Cusentino, a bar-tender, was sleeping upstairs. One night he was awakened in the middle of the night by a man in his 60's wear-ing pajamas and a bathrobe, who angrily stared down at him be-fore disappearing.

The Willow Hotel after the last fire.

Then, late one winter night Kevin Mooney, part owner of the restaurant, was locking up when a glimpse out the back window stopped him cold. "There were these two beet-red eyes staring back at me," he recalled. "I never saw anything like it. Finally I got up nerve enough to open the door, but it wouldn't move. Seems like it took hours to get it open. Once I did, there was no one — *nothing* there."

It wasn't the end. Tom Thorton and Steve Hagel, caretakers of the gutted building, spent several fearsome nights as the very walls seemed to take on a frightening will of their own. "There were weird, wild noises—nothing that we could identify, nothing human," they attempted to explain later.

Though the hotel itself was never rebuilt, the building, still known as the Willow Hotel, continues as a restaurant and bar. Patrons and employees alike report seeing "a frizzy redhead," believed to be Elualah Sims who was murdered by her husband in the bar nearly 100 years ago. There's another apparition as well, a small, furtive man who wanders through the halls as though searching for someone.

And yet another ghost frequently appears who looks like a gambler straight from central casting complete with dapper mustache and immaculate black suit. He's more aggressive than the other spirits, appearing at the bar—only to disappear when served. Look around next time you're in the area, perhaps he'll deal you a hand.

The Willow Hotel is located on the corner of Main and Willow streets in Jamestown. Telephone: (209) 984-3998.

Anita and Francis Laney live in a Marysville Victorian manor house that looks like a frosty pink wedding cake. The architectural confection seems like the antithesis of the Charles Addams

THE LANEY HOUSE

haunt—yet a whole family of spirits resides there.

The Laneys bought the place in 1962, little dreaming what was in store for them. "The previous owners had no contact whatsoever with anything supernatural," Anita says. "Three years passed uneventfully. Then we began to be aware of a presence in the house. I'd come in the back door and hear music. 'Who left the stereo on?' I'd wonder. The answer was—no one. The stereo wasn't on. The music was coming from another world.

"Then the Republican women wanted to have a tea at the house. I came home from the office to get the kitchen cleaned up for them. I was rushed and not in the best mood when I heard a man's footsteps behind me. I thought, 'Oh, hell!' certain that it was my husband wanting lunch.

"'What are you doing here?' I asked without turning. There was no answer, yet I could feel someone standing just behind me. When I turned at last I found that the kitchen was empty."

One night Anita switched off the bedside lamp and settled back, only to be confronted by the head and shoulders of a man floating above the marble-topped dresser. She turned the light back on and it was gone, turned it off again and this time saw a full length form of a man.

"I knew exactly who it was," Anita says. "Norman Abbott Rideout— first owner of the house. I recognized him because he's a younger version of his father, Norman Danning Rideout, the prominent Gold Country banker of the last century—I'd seen his picture many times. I knew that the elder Rideout had built the house as a wedding gift for his son in 1885.

The Laney House. Photograph by A. May.

"Eleven years later the young husband and father was the sole victim in a mine disaster. I'm certain that it's this man whom I saw then and have seen again many times over the years."

The Laneys believe that the house is haunted not only by Norman but by his wife and children as well. "We hear their voices and footsteps often and sometimes catch glimpses of them as well," Francis explains. "There's a little boy and a pretty little girl with long blond hair—she resembles her grandfather."

"Norman and his wife are very fashionably dressed," Anita adds. "She's quite beautiful. I see her standing at the window often. They seem like such a happy family. Maybe that's why they stay here; possibly they're living out the happy times they shared in this house. It reminds me of the ghost in Our Town who came back to relive one day. Maybe they've chosen to remain here for all eternity. That would be a kind of heaven, now wouldn't it?"

Footsteps are the most common phenomenon experienced by the Laneys and their guests. One evening Anita was entertaining a branch of the American Association of University Women.

"We had just heard a review of the Edgar Cayce biography, *There Is A River,* and I was serving refreshments when we all heard the front door open," Anita recalls.   "Guess the movie's out, sounds like Fran coming home," one woman said.

"But Fran didn't come in to say hello. Instead the steps went clomping on up the stairs. I called out to him and when he didn't answer I went to investigate. Nobody was there.

"Just a few minutes later a guest cried out as her spoon tore itself out of her hand and flew across the room. Somebody was there but it certainly wasn't Fran!"

The first time the Laneys heard spectral voices they were startled, but over the years have grown accustomed to them—with one exception. As Anita was bathing one morning, she heard a woman call out from downstairs.   Then a man's voice answered—from right there in the bathroom. "I leaped out of the tub and grabbed a towel," Anita says. "Ghost or no ghost, I don't like the idea of a strange man in the bathroom with me!"

Anita believes that the ghosts are keeping an eye on her in more ways than one. "They have their little methods of telling me they think I'm doing too much, getting involved in too many projects. One night— morning really, it was three a. m. — I was sitting on the floor surrounded by big rolls of newsprint.   Though awfully tired, I felt obligated to complete a club assignment that I'd undertaken, a decorating project.

"I heard footsteps quite clearly descending the stairs.   I thought it was Fran and I was so determined to finish that I didn't say a word. The steps reached the foot of the stairs, walked down the hall and across the living room. Finally they were right behind me. I turned at last and saw—no one. Well, when it gets so bad that a ghost has to come and tell

THE MOTHER LODE COUNTRY

you to slow down, you begin to get the message. I got up and went to bed."

The ghosts sometimes appear a bit like animals misbehaving when their humans are away. "Once a young couple was staying in the house while we were on vacation," Anita recalls. "While sitting in the living room, they heard a terrific crash upstairs. Upon investigating, they found that two tall vases and an antique compote had fallen off a shelf.

"Our young friends were terribly upset when we got back. 'We just can't explain it,' they kept saying. I could explain it well enough. I went upstairs and said aloud, 'This doesn't please me at all. I'm very disappointed.' I left the pieces on the floor for six weeks as a kind of reminder. It hasn't happened again."

But coexisting with ghosts is a two-way street, Anita admits. "If we don't hear from them for a while, we get worried. What if they should go away! Sometimes I ask, 'Are you angry with me? I'm sorry if I've done anything to displease you.' Sometimes I've even pleaded, 'Come back!'

"And they always do."

The Laney House is located at 710 D St., in Marysville.

Anita Laney. Photograph by C.J. Marrow

I long to talk with some
old lover's ghost,
Who died before the god
of love was born.

— John Donne